If you have a child struggling with mental illn... ...ting down with a good friend who can relate t... and has much wisdom to share. It's not a succ... ...ng is neatly tied in a bow at the end, but it is a story of hope in a great and loving God who holds our lives in His hands. Reading this book will encourage you and spur you on to persevere in the midst of difficulty, keeping your eyes fixed on Christ, the one who suffered for us.

KERI FOLMAR
Author of the *Delighting in the Word Bible Study* series and *The Good Portion: Scripture* and cohost of Priscilla Talk

A brother-in-law isn't typically an impartial reader. So why endorse this book? For years I watched up close as Leslie and Steve rejoiced, cried, fought, fell down, and got back up again. Leslie captured this journey brilliantly within these pages. It's a story of courage and trust that all parents would benefit from, not just adoptive parents. The story is not sugar-coated. Disney would never consider an ending like theirs. Brace yourself, reader, and learn from experience to rest in the Lord.

MATT SCHMUCKER
Elder, Capitol Hill Baptist Church in Washington, DC;
Director, CROSS Conference (www.crosscon.com)

How do you keep going when your world is falling apart? Leslie Schmucker has written an accessible, authentic, hopeful book about clinging to God and His promises in the midst of the hardest, most painful circumstances a family could face. This book isn't just for families experiencing mental health issues; it is for anyone enduring severe suffering and desperate for hope.

JOHN KNIGHT
Donor Officer, Desiring God

This book is amazing. Truly. Never have I read a book that so powerfully owns the heart-wrenching realities of raising a child with severe mental illness, while simultaneously and fervently pointing the reader to truths of Scripture, the power of the gospel, and the love of God in Christ. I couldn't put the book down. Everyone should read this book – for the painfully honest picture it conveys of the realities of family life when severe mental illness is present – and for the crystal-clear hope it points us to in Christ, whatever our challenges may be. Leslie Schmucker has hit a home run!

STEPHANIE O. HUBACH
Author, *Same Lake, Different Boat: Coming Alongside People Touched by Disability*, and *Parenting & Disabilities: Abiding in God's Presence*,
Research Fellow, Disability Ministries,
Covenant Theological Seminary, St. Louis, Missouri

BROKEN CHILDREN
SOVEREIGN GOD
REJOICING IN GOD'S GOODNESS
AMIDST CHILDHOOD MENTAL HEALTH STRUGGLES

LESLIE SCHMUCKER

CHRISTIAN
FOCUS

Copyright © Leslie Schmucker 2023

Paperback ISBN 978-1-5271-1013-7

E-book ISBN 978-1-5271-1071-7

10 9 8 7 6 5 4 3 2 1

Published in 2023
by
Christian Focus Publications Ltd,
Geanies House, Fearn, Ross-shire,
IV20 1TW, Great Britain.

www.christianfocus.com

Cover design by
Alistair MacInnes

Printed by
Bell & Bain, Glasgow

CONTENTS

Acknowledgments 7

Introduction 9

SECTION ONE
Comfort from the God Who Knows

Chapter One: Loneliness and Isolation 17

Chapter Two: Doubt and Confusion 25

Chapter Three: Grief 33

Chapter Four: Guilt and Shame 41

Chapter Five: Fear 49

SECTION TWO
God's Sufficiency in the Fallout

Chapter Six: The Effects of Mental Illness
     on Siblings 59

Chapter Seven: The Effects of Mental Illness
     on Marriage 67

Chapter Eight: Falsely Accused 75

Chapter Nine: Dredging Up the Past 83

SECTION THREE
Guidance in the Storm

Chapter Ten: Gospel Grace 93

Chapter Eleven: Releasing Children to Christ 103

Chapter Twelve: Navigating the System 111

Chapter Thirteen: Finding Identity in Christ 119

Chapter Fourteen: Finding a Support System 129

Chapter Fifteen: Helping Children Fight Fear 137

Chapter Sixteen: Message for the Church 145

SECTION FOUR
Hope for the Journey

Chapter Seventeen: Beautiful Narrative 157

To
Steve

James 1:12

Acknowledgments

The Teacher said, 'But woe to him who is alone when he falls and has not another to lift him up' (Eccles. 4:10)! He wasn't kidding. Raising our daughter was a team effort, and an exercise in humility and gratitude. In other words, I couldn't have persevered through this trial without the following folks.

First, my husband, Steve. If refining in fire makes metal shine, then you are radiant. Your perseverance and wisdom throughout Jackie's childhood were unmatched, and I am grateful that God matched us to be her parents.

Michael and Alison Schmucker, Claire and Matt Henry, you stepped up in the sibling and in-law sibling department. You cared for Jackie when it was hard, which blessed your father and me. Claire, you get a double acknowledgment, because you bore the brunt on the front lines. And now you are a grown woman who has come through the fire with forgiveness and fortitude. Well done, you, Baby Girl. Well, Michael, I should mention your amazing spinning bear hugs which made Jackie giggle and the rest of us smile.

To Deb and Darryl Bodine and Betsy Echternach, who very graciously read and revised many pages of early iterations of this book, as well as other projects. Plus, you are the sweetest of friends. You're living proof that a 'joyful heart is good medicine' (Prov. 17:22). And Deb, your care of Jackie and me was a sweet balm. Thank you.

For the folks who were willing to offer us respite and rest, even when your property was destroyed in the process or your bunny got some high jumps on the trampoline – Luke and Mindy Morrie, Joel and Jackie Frey, the Osman family, Gretta Williams, Debbie Greenawalt, and Jim and Marsha Schmucker. Jackie loves all of you, and so do I.

Matt Schmucker, in addition to persistently sharing the gospel with Steve and me back in 1984, I am so very grateful for your connections. Without your gracious email introductions, I couldn't be thanking you for your role in this book right now.

To my encouragers. Kathy Antol and Laura Weidensaul, my oldest friends, who gave me double the listening ear. Mary Stauffer, I'm so glad for our 'Groma' connection, and your patient and compassionate endurance of the trials that rocked our family. For my brother, Tim Breen, who still calls me 'Sissy,' which melts my heart. You and I have been through it, and are living proof of Christ's faithfulness.

For Dayspring Christian Academy, who gave four and a half years of educating Jackie a try. You truly live up to your philosophy of partnering with parents.

To the prayer warriors and servants at Grace Baptist Church, particularly the pastors, Joel DeVinney and Scott Harrison. You are truly Christ's body.

To Jackie, who has put her stamp of approval on this book. You have persevered through so much, and are persevering still. Dad and I love you and always will.

And, of course, to Jesus.

Introduction

The fall of man altered every atom of creation. From manhood to motherhood to matrimony, nothing is as it should be. Some after-effects of the fall are mere annoyances, like the fear of spiders, or indigestion, or having to wear uncomfortable clothing. But most by-products of the fall take the breath from your lungs, wrench your heart from your chest, and are counted in tears. Childhood mental illness is one of those by-products.

According to the American Academy of Family Physicians (AAFP), one in six American children between the ages of six and seventeen have a diagnosed mental health disorder, the most prevalent of which include anxiety, depression, and attention deficit hyperactivity disorder (ADHD).[1] The CDC reports that suicide is the second leading cause of death among American children aged ten to fourteen.[2] Mental Health America reports that between 2020 and 2021, there was a 13 percent increase in cases of children experiencing major depressive episodes.[3] That is 206,000 children in the United States alone. Whether these increases are due to broader

---

1. Michael Devitt, 'Study: One in Six U.S. Children Has a Mental Illness' (American Academy of Family Physicians: March 18, 2019), aafp.org/news/ health-of-the-public/20190318childmentalillness

2. 'Suicide' (National Institute of Mental Health. U.S. Department of Health and Human Services). Accessed August 1, 2022. nimh.nih.gov/health/statistics/ suicide

3. '2020 Mental Health in America – Youth Data' (Mental Health America, Inc., 2022). mhanational.org/issues/2020/mental-health-america-youth-data

screening methods or an actual rise in cases, it remains that a significant number of American households are affected by varying degrees of childhood mental illness.

The World Health Organization reports similar statistics globally, claiming that 'mental health conditions account for 16 percent of the global burden of disease and injury in people aged ten to nineteen years.'[4] It reports that up to 20 percent of children worldwide are diagnosed with a mental health disorder, with half of those disorders manifesting by age fourteen. Globally, suicide is the third leading cause of death in children aged fifteen to nineteen years. More than half of these children do not receive treatment for their disorders.

These alarming statistics play out in the small Christian school where I teach, as well as in schools across the nation. In the last few years alone, my school has seen an alarming rise in self-harm, psychiatric hospitalizations, suicidal thoughts, and students who are unable to leave their home to come to school because of varying degrees of anxiety. I have sat next to a student who was retching in a trash can because of a debilitating panic attack. I have met students at their parents' car to talk them through simply coming into the building. Our school has come alongside parents in helping to unlock the mystery of intense irrational fear or profound and stifling sadness. Christian families are not immune from the scourge of childhood mental illness.

There are myriad reasons for the uptick in mental health challenges among our children. We can point to social media, Covid, a removal of prayer and Bible reading from the schools, fatherlessness, or disastrous government policies. But no matter the cause, the fallout has left thousands of families in despair, confusion, and impotent desperation.

---

4. 'Adolescent and Young Adult Health' (World Health Organization, January 18, 2021). who.int/news-room/fact-sheets/detail/adolescents-health-risks-and-solutions

If you are raising a child who is stricken with mental illness, whether your child is adopted or biological, you may know the heartache, intensity, and uncertainty of the day to day, and the helplessness and frustration of navigating a life full of disconnects in logic, embarrassing behavior, and fear for the future. God sees you, He knows you and your child, and He shares your pain. He is sovereign, He is good, and He has not left us alone in our affliction.

My Story

In the world of public special education, childhood mental illness is termed Emotional Disturbance, and classrooms designed to teach children with mental illness are termed Emotional Support. I taught in such classrooms for the first fourteen years of my career, which to date spans almost four decades. I love how God works, even though often you can't see it until you have the gift of hindsight. I never expected to teach children with mental illness. What began as a foot in the door to teaching ended up becoming a passion and love for children who are seen as bizarre, are often violent, perennially anxious, rarely trusting, and perpetually marginalized. If 'the Lord is near to the broken hearted' (Ps. 34:18), He was certainly working in my classroom.

Over those fourteen years in emotional support classrooms, I worked with a motley myriad of students. I witnessed the heartache of abuse, abandonment, and generational recurrences of madness. Many of my classrooms were permeated with violence, physical restraints, and regular disruption. Early in my career, classrooms for emotionally disturbed children did not make the distinction between diagnoses, severity of disorders, or even ages of the students. One of my first classrooms was comprised of twelve boys, ranging in age from six through twelve, with diagnoses that ranged from autism to oppositional defiant disorder to psychosis. Included on the class list were a towering and violent sixth grader who was two inches taller than I was, a twelve-year-old rapist, an eight-year-old lanky and aggressive boy with an intellectual disability and a very foul mouth, and a tiny meek and withdrawn first grader with autism. I had one diminutive assistant, who was easily forty years my senior, and a head full of book learning. And though at the time of my first classroom I didn't know Him yet, I had a God who was working mightily on my behalf.

Our Story

For the first twelve years of my career, I was a churchgoer, but not a believer. In midsummer of 1997, a woman introduced Henry Blackaby's Bible study, *Experiencing God*, to our church.[5] My husband, Steve, and I both participated, and what we learned placed our wandering feet squarely on the path to Christ. In the pages of Blackaby's study, I read a truth so profound that I lingered on the words, returning to them again and again: 'No one can come to me unless the Father who sent me draws him' (John 6:44). As we learned more about God, the work of Christ on the cross, and hungered more and more for His Word, I suddenly understood that we were being drawn in by God Himself! The first scripture we memorized for the study was John 15:5, 'I am the vine; you are the branches. Whoever abides in me and I in him, he it is that bears much fruit, for apart from me you can do nothing.' The relief that resulted from the truth of that verse grabbed hold of me in an ineffable grip of love and comfort. Keith Getty's preeminent and illustrious modern hymn *In Christ Alone* captures what was happening in my heart as I read those refreshing truths: 'What heights of love, what depths of peace, when fears are stilled, when strivings cease, my Comforter, my All in All, here in the love of Christ I stand.'[6]

---

5. Claude V. King and Henry T. Blackaby, *Experiencing God: Knowing and Doing the Will of God; Leader's Guide* (Nashville, TN: LifeWay Press, 1999).

6. Keith and Kristyn Getty, *In Christ Alone* (MP3. Getty Music, n.d.).

Finding God's Sovereignty in the Midst of Childhood Mental Illness

On a chilly April Tuesday morning, twenty-two years after my first encounter with childhood mental illness, and ten years after Jesus Christ took hold of my husband and me, I got on my knees and confessed to God that my walk with Him was too comfortable. I asked Him to show me a way my husband and I might stretch the limits of our comfort zone, to be better contributors to His kingdom. My husband is fond of saying, 'Be careful what you pray for,' because the outcome of that prayer eventually propelled us down a road we never imagined we'd be traveling. At first, the entrance to the road seemed miraculously paved, clearly marked, wide, and exciting. However, the speed bumps, yield signs, potholes, construction zones, speed traps, shoulderless cliffsides, and tortuous curves we eventually encountered left us weary, haggard, and often looking for the nearest exit ramp. Much of our journey was spent white-knuckled and clinging in fear and desperation to our Father and Guide.

When God placed me in that first classroom for emotionally disturbed children, I had no idea He was preparing my family and me for the adoption of our daughter Jackie. I couldn't have known that the violence and mayhem, joys and victories in my classrooms were all boot camp for bringing mental illness into our home.

When we were raising our daughter, the intensity of feelings that ran rampant and overtook our lives ranged from joy, to hope, to intense isolation, to shame, to confusion, and even to feelings of outright insanity. Trying to navigate a broken system, being accused (more than once) of child abuse, receiving regular phone calls and emails from school, endless counseling sessions, trying (and failing) to find the one right intervention that would finally cure our daughter, and living in a house where chaos and hostility prevailed, all took their toll.

13

But, through it all, we found comfort from a steady, present, loving God who could relate to the trials we were experiencing. And so we clung to Him with all we had, because He was all we had. And He didn't disappoint. His love has never failed, and His sovereignty and goodness are as sure as the change of seasons.

This book is my effort to showcase a good God in a broken world, even a world that crushes the lives of little kids, and leaves parents heartbroken and wanting. Or to put it another way, I desire to exalt God in the lowest points in our lives, to testify to His sufficiency and goodness, and to show that our good and noble desires in what He calls us to are penultimate to what must be our highest and primary desire: God Himself.

SECTION ONE

Comfort from the God Who Knows

1

Loneliness and Isolation

I stood in the candy aisle a few days before Easter, trying desperately to focus. I knew what each of my children liked in their baskets. Peanut butter cups for Claire. Snickers for Michael. Skittles for Matt, Claire's husband, and salted caramel for Alison, Michael's wife. Jackie liked Sour Patch Kids. This annual errand usually elicited great joy and anticipation, but this year was different. There seemed to be too many choices, the lights above me were too bright, the people around me too distant. I felt somehow detached from my experience. The labels on the candy bars shimmied and danced through my tears, my mind so locked up it wouldn't let me distinguish one brand from the next. Never before, or since, have I ever been so utterly trapped in such a fog of loneliness and isolation. I stood frozen to the spot, disconnected from everything around me, hugging my arms in a vice grip, gently rocking back and forth. 'Help me, Lord,' I whispered.

The Savior Who Knows

If you are raising a child who is mentally ill, you may feel lonely, even in a crowd of other parents, even, and sometimes especially, in your church. There is no frame of reference for raising a child who is afflicted, no parenting manual, no tidy method or intervention. Even parents of so-called 'strong willed' children cannot begin to imagine the stress and chaos of the day to day. I have heard multiple stories of parents who were left alone by friends, family, and their church because no one knew what to do with or for them. Loneliness and isolation can become the norm. Praise God we have a Savior who knows what it is like to be alone.

Walmart at Easter is no Gethsemane,[1] but I knew that crying out to Christ in the midst of my desolation in that store would not fall on deaf ears because of His own few days before Easter. No, I was not going to bear the weight of all humanity, but I was living in a torrent of chaos and violence, police visits and counseling sessions, stealing and cutting, and marriage-crushing stress that often left me withered with despair and hopelessness. I knew Jesus could relate.

Picture Him in the garden. He has just completed His earthly ministry, teaching and preaching to His lost sheep, and preparing His little band of men, those thick fellows who were often slow on the uptake and had no clue why they were following Him. He must have been exhausted. His ministry was urgent and all-consuming, and not always fruitful. And He knew how it would end. Even though He understood what lay beyond that first Good Friday, that promised 'joy set before him' (Heb. 12:2),[2] His humanness led Him to fear the physical pain and utter desolation He was about to face. He was surrounded by people, yet isolated and friendless. He did not 'entrust himself to them … for he himself knew what was in man' (John 2:24-25). And there in the garden, when He needed His disciples the most, He found them sleeping.[3]

Perhaps you can relate. Your child is not like other children. Your parenting does not and cannot remotely resemble that of your friends with typical children, so they cannot identify

---

1. Matthew 26:36: 'Then Jesus went with them to a place called Gethsemane, and he said to his disciples, "Sit here, while I go over there and pray."'

2. '[L]ooking to Jesus, the founder and perfecter of our faith, who for the joy that was set before him endured the cross, despising the shame, and is seated at the right hand of the throne of God.'

3. Matthew 26:40 'And he came to the disciples and found them sleeping. And he said to Peter, "So, could you not watch with me one hour?"'

with you and you can't explain it to them. Every outing, every family visit, every day is a calculated, mapped out plan for getting through without mayhem or embarrassment. Even if you have a wonderful system of support, you still are alone in your experience.

Jesus was profoundly alone in His experience too. He had no confidant. No counselor, no close friend to call in the middle of the night to share in what He was feeling. He had no one to relate to, and no one could relate to Him. Standing accused before the Sanhedrin, facing an incredulous assessment by Pontius Pilate, enduring the scoffing curiosity of Herod, listening to the mocking of the Roman guards, feeling their spit on His face, stumbling along the Via Dolorosa beneath the heavy crossbeam and the crowd's staring eyes, ascending Calvary, and submitting to being nailed hand and foot to a tree, He was alone. For the first and only time in eternity, Christ was forsaken, isolated, and without help. He cried out, 'My God, why have you forsaken me?' (Matt. 27:46).

For all He endured, and in His most lonesome moments, Jesus never stopped crying out to His Father. And His pleas were no eloquent, censored prayers. They were raw, pleading, and audacious laments for help and relief. Face to the ground, He pleaded, 'Father, if it be possible, let this cup pass' (Matt. 26:39). Writhing in agony on the cross, He searched in prayer for His Father, wondering, 'Why?' I don't know how long Jesus felt forsaken by God, but even the shortest possible increment of time would have been too long. Yet He never stopped praying. He never stopped reaching out for help from God. And knowing He could have at any time called down an army of angels to relieve Him from the ordeal, instead, fueled by great love and unfathomable grace, He prayed for forgiveness for the ignorant creatures for whom He was bearing this agony. 'Forgive them,' He pleaded. 'They know not what they do' (Luke 23:34).

Then it was finished. And in the finishing came our rescue, and our permission to cry to Him with our own raw and audacious lament.

The Word Used the Word

Despite my faith in Him, I sometimes struggle with the invisibility of God. When I pray, I can tend to feel alone, and doubt that He is listening, because I can see nothing tangible to affirm His presence. After a loud and angry evening with our daughter, or yet another phone call from the school, or after finding the umpteenth stolen electronic device in her room, or another parent has called complaining about our daughter's harassment of their child, the loneliness and isolation would set in, and I'd go inward. Praying seemed elusive at times, because the cacophony of our lives drowned out the still, small voice of my Savior.

Maybe you have felt the same. You pray. You plead and ask for relief. But there is silence on the other end. You become tempted to believe that God isn't really there. The loneliness is compounded.

When Satan tried to convince Jesus to forget His Father in the wilderness, Christ was alone, hungry, and sleep-deprived.[4] Being fully human, I'm sure He was vulnerable to the attack. Yet He counterattacked with, ironically enough, His own words. Satan knew how to land a strategically placed scripture, but he was dealing with the Word Himself! So, if the author of salvation, the very Word of God used this tactic, so should we.

When you are tempted to forget the omnipresence and benevolence of God because your life is louder than His voice, use the megaphone of Scripture to drown out the clamor of the trial.

---

4. Matthew 4:1-2: 'Then Jesus was led up by the Spirit into the wilderness to be tempted by the devil. And after fasting forty days and forty nights, he was hungry.'

For his invisible attributes, namely, his eternal power and divine nature, have been clearly perceived, ever since the creation of the world, in the things that have been made. So they are without excuse. (Rom. 1:20)

And this is the confidence that we have toward him, that if we ask anything according to his will he hears us. (1 John 5:14)

If anyone is a worshiper of God and does his will, God listens to him. (John 9:31)

For the eyes of the Lord are on the righteous, and his ears are open to their prayer. (1 Pet. 3:12)

Let us then with confidence draw near to the throne of grace, that we may receive mercy and find grace to help in time of need. (Heb. 4:16)

I have learned to meditate on His Word when I am feeling alone. Jesus Christ has left us little room to doubt His existence and His care for us. Because of Christ's finished work on the cross we can, indeed, 'draw near to his throne of grace' with confidence and boldness. Like the angels, who have full access to the throne room, we too can walk, with humility and reverence, into the presence of God.[5] We are told to draw near to him. And what is the outcome of our drawing near? Incredibly, He draws near to us (Jas. 4:8)![6] The King of the universe draws near to me in my loneliness to show His abounding love for me. Though my situation doesn't change, my countenance does, and I am helped.

---

5. Job 1:6: 'Now there was a day when the sons of God came to present themselves before the LORD, and Satan also came among them.'

6. 'Draw near to God, and he will draw near to you. Cleanse your hands, you sinners, and purify your hearts, you double-minded.'

I included Romans 1:20 in this list, because I have also found that meditating on the magnificence of nature helps me ground myself in the reality of God's existence, and I feel His presence even more sharply. When I doubt, I consider, for example, the enormous pine tree in my backyard. It is old and massive, yet somehow it takes water from the ground, and in a great gravity-defying feat, brings it all the way to the highest most branches without pump or vacuum. Incredible. Yesterday, I stopped to watch hundreds of honey bees busily gathering nectar from the lovely little white flowers that have bloomed all across the vine on our fence. I pondered how those bees were designed for the very purpose of pollinating those flowers so they could be enjoyed year after year. Or, how about the fact that I have grown human beings *inside my body*? When I consider the wonder, majesty, grandeur, minutiae, vastness, intricacy, opulence, and sublimity of creation, I see the genius of the Creator, and I am convinced once more that He exists, which comforts me in my loneliness.

His Rod and His Staff Will Comfort

Perhaps one of the most illustrative examples of Christ's care and constant nearness in our lives is the depiction of Him as a shepherd. Shepherds are utterly dedicated to their flock in a way that is all-consuming in their lives. Consider all the times God refers to Christ as our shepherd and to us as His sheep:

> The Lord is my shepherd; I shall not want. He makes me lie down in green pastures. He leads me beside still waters. He restores my soul. He leads me in paths of righteousness for his name's sake. Even though I walk through the valley of the shadow of death, I will fear no evil, for you are with me; your rod and your staff, they comfort me. (Ps. 23:1-4)

> I am the good shepherd. I know my own and my own know me. (John 10:14)

> When he saw the crowds, he had compassion for them, because they were harassed and helpless, like sheep without a shepherd. (Matt. 9:36)

> He will tend his flock like a shepherd; he will gather the lambs in his arms; he will carry them in his bosom, and gently lead those that are with young. (Isa. 40:11)

> What man of you, having a hundred sheep, if he has lost one of them, does not leave the ninety-nine in the open country, and go after the one that is lost, until he finds it? And when he has found it, he lays it on his shoulders, rejoicing. (Luke 15:3-5)

In Bible times, shepherding was a 24/7 affair. If you were a shepherd, that's all you were. You did more than feed and water your sheep. You cared for their health and protected them from parasites and predators. You slept with them in the field at night, keeping a wary eye out for wild beasts. Making them lie down meant you were seeing to it that your sheep were relaxed. Stressed sheep tend to wander, and they don't want to eat. Or, if they are hungry, they will roam and roam in search of food. A good shepherd will make his sheep lie still so they can rest and receive nourishment. Moving water will stop a sheep in its tracks, so shepherds need to lead them to still water in order for them to ford a stream or drink from it. The oil spoken of in Psalm 23:5 was more than symbolic.[7] Shepherds would routinely rub oil on their sheep's heads to protect them from insects. Parasites could be extremely uncomfortable or even

---

7. 'You prepare a table before me in the presence of my enemies; you anoint my head with oil; my cup overflows.'

deadly for sheep. The rod and staff were used as guides, but also as prods. Both uses gave comfort, even if they sometimes were uncomfortable, because they kept the sheep together. Sheep don't survive well on their own.

The Bible uses this beautiful imagery to remind us that God is always with us, even in our loneliest moments. We are His sheep, and He cares about every detail of our life.

In my church growing up, the front of the sanctuary was dominated by an enormous stained glass window depicting a larger than life Christ, tenderly hefting a sweet lamb across His shoulders. I loved that window, and still think of that image today. I like to imagine I am that lamb. What great comfort to know that Jesus is a 24/7 shepherd who looks on me with compassion, knows me, will find me when I'm lost, and, when I'm lonely, gently lead me back to His bosom where I'll find comfort and rest.

The Bosom of the Savior

My heart aches when I think about Jesus in the garden – because He endured so much for me – and for you. Nothing we experience in life, not even the extreme level of loneliness that living with a child with mental illness brings, can come close to the loneliness Jesus suffered for you and for me on that first Easter. There are promises in the Bible we can stand on, boldly and with solid assurance because we have a Savior who can empathize with us. We are never alone.

I went home from Walmart that day with a few bags of candy and a settled peace. I knew I was going home to the tumult, but I was going in the bosom of my Savior, armed with His promises to draw near to me in my loneliness. It was a good Easter.

2
Doubt and Confusion

A few years ago I received a series of tragic updates that tipped my normally trust-filled, hope-saturated prayers into anguished cries of lament. A very close friend's pre-teen daughter had suddenly and inexplicably fallen into the darkness of mental illness, thrusting her bewildered parents into the disorienting world of the mental health system. Another dear friend's son and daughter-in-law had just lost their third baby girl to a genetic disorder. And a local pastor's tiny daughter contracted E. coli at a county fair, leaving her with debilitating behavioral and physical health challenges. All of it compounded our grief and confusion over the loss of our daughter Jackie, who had recently chosen to begin life with her infant daughter homeless in Philadelphia, rather than coming home to our family.

Why Lord?

For the first time in my life I prayed through gritted teeth, 'Thy will be done.' How Lord, I mewled, is this good for the kingdom? Why, Father, would you place a beautiful child of a couple who has served you faithfully their whole lives, in a psychiatric facility? How is taking yet another child from a couple whose faith is tenuous going to bring them to trust in you? What good can come from inflicting a three-year-old with pain and permanent damage, even as her father is shepherding your people? Why, Lord, have you not cured our daughter's mental illness, despite the love and care we have given her?

It is confusing when serving God ends in trial. Our experience with Jackie couldn't have been further from our hopes. Though there were times when we were optimistic about our daughter, the aggression, social-service investigations, police visits, hospitalizations, endless counseling sessions, stealing, running away, and chaos that often pervaded our home during the nearly nine years she lived with us ultimately left us with more questions than answers.

God, we wondered, did we not ask for success with our daughter? Did we not seek your face at every turn when we were raising her? Did we not desperately pound on the door of your grace with every challenge and crisis we faced? The daughter God blessed us with rejected us at every turn, and ultimately left our home without looking back. We wondered if God's promises had failed.

When my husband and I prayed over and for our daughter, we boldly asked God to save her from the effects of the trauma and turbulence of her formative years. We were specific. Lord, please give us wisdom to help Jackie bridle her temper. Father, please give Jackie good success in school. Abba, please be with us in today's counseling session, because it's going to be a rough one. We had a hopeful expectation that God would fulfill the words of Matthew 7, but we felt instead like we had asked and not been given, sought and not found, knocked and encountered only a barrier between us and our daughter.[1]

When Jackie came into our lives, we were certain that God had brought her to us. We adopted her and loved her as our own. She had full access to all that our biological children have. She is ours. We gave her our name and a place in our family. We poured nine long and difficult years into her life, often

---

1. Matthew 7:7-8: 'Ask, and it will be given to you; seek, and you will find; knock, and it will be opened to you. For everyone who asks receives, and the one who seeks finds, and to the one who knocks it will be opened.'

sacrificing the needs of our other children. Time, resources, and stamina were nearly exhausted by the time she had left. But the fruit we were sure we would see never materialized. We had failed. What, we wondered, was God thinking?

I did not sense bitterness in our lament, only earnest questioning from our tattered hearts. Still, I wondered if we had veered into dangerous territory. Were we being like Job's wife? Were we cursing God (Job 2:9)?[2]

What Was God Thinking?

When doubt and confusion befall God's children, we want to know why. And we are in excellent company. 'Why have you forsaken me?' asks David, and later, quoting him, Jesus (Ps. 22:1; Mark 15:34). Habakkuk wonders, 'Why do you make me see iniquity, and why do you idly look at wrong?' (Hab. 1:3). And then there's Job, who, after wishing he would have died at birth, complains:

> Why is light given to a man whose way is hidden, whom God has hedged in? For my sighing comes instead of my bread, and my groanings are poured out like water. For the thing that I fear comes upon me, and what I dread befalls me. I am not at ease, nor am I quiet; I have no rest, but trouble comes. (Job 3:23-26)

God allows, even encourages, faith-filled laments and queries from His people. Our status as children (John 1:12)[3] and heirs (Rom. 8:17)[4] enables us to come to Him with confidence and wide-eyed inquiry. We must take care, however, not to cross the line from faith-filled lament into doubting God's goodness.

---

2. 'Then his wife said to him, "Do you still hold fast your integrity? Curse God and die."'

3. 'But to all who did receive him, who believed in his name he gave the right to become children of God.'

4. 'and if children, then heirs – heirs of God and fellow heirs with Christ, provided we suffer with him in order that we may also be glorified with him.'

In the months and years since our daughter left, my husband and I have questioned whether or not we heard God correctly when He brought Jackie into our lives. Our recent conclusion is that we may have been looking for fruit on the wrong tree. The obvious reason for adopting a child is their salvation, both physically and, for the Christian family, spiritually. But God doesn't often deal in the obvious. I could posit myriad reasons for God's putting our daughter in our life. The fruit we had so hoped for could very possibly still be a tiny seed, or a shoot that is planted in some distant forest waiting to give shade to someone who has been touched by our story. Maybe it was on the tree of our marriage, or our sanctification, or our daughter's journey toward Christ. What was God thinking? I have no idea. We thought we were so sure, but 'who has known the mind of the Lord?' (Rom. 11:34). So our question was all wrong. Not 'what was God thinking,' but rather, 'what does God say?'

God is Still Good

J. I. Packer, in his marvelous book *Knowing God,* addresses our tendency to 'feel sure that God has enabled us to understand all His ways with us, and to be able to see at once the reason for anything that may happen to us in the future.' He writes:

> And then something very painful and quite inexplicable comes along, and our cheerful illusion of being in God's secret counsels is shattered. Our pride is wounded; we feel that God has slighted us; and unless at this point we repent and humble ourselves very thoroughly for our former presumption, our whole subsequent spiritual life may be blighted.[5]

We thought we knew what God was doing. The painful results of our daughter's mental illness and subsequent failed adoption,

---

5. J. I. Packer, 'Chapter Ten: God's Wisdom and Ours,' *Knowing God* (Downers Grove, IL: InterVarsity Press, 1993), p. 106.

however, reminded us that God is God and we are not. We know without a doubt that God is good. We know that He loves us, and that He has perfect and trustworthy reasons for having brought our daughter into our lives and turning our existence on its head. How do we know this? Because of what He has said in His Word. And we believe Him. We have no choice. We have been laid bare. So, in looking for answers, we breathlessly declare with Peter, 'Lord, to whom shall we go? You have the words of eternal life, and we have believed, and have come to know, that you are the Holy One of God' (John 6:68-69).

Only God's Word has the answers to our questions about His intentions in our lives, and it is the only source for searching for His light when darkness encroaches. God's narrow road is not easy.[6] Christ telling us His burden is easy and His yoke is light is not a promise of a stress-free existence here on earth.[7] It is a promise that He will lift the burden we don't need to bear anymore, our sin. It is a promise of a future glory and of provision in the midst of trials today.

When you carefully study God's promises and take Him at His word, a beautiful narrative begins to form. After listening to God's voice in the Scriptures, my husband and I have concluded that though we have spent nine of our thirty-eight years together in utter stress and chaos, and though our marriage nearly ended, and though our child is lost to us today, God is still good. He still loves us, and Christ's burdens, indeed, are lighter than anything we can experience in our temporal lives. The burdens of life overwhelm us with the weight of the world. The suffering of Jesus Christ offers us the far greater 'eternal weight of glory' (2 Cor. 4:17).[8]

---

6. Matthew 7:14: 'For the gate is narrow and the way is hard that leads to life, and those who find it are few.'

7. Matthew 11:30: 'For my yoke is easy, and my burden is light.'

8. 'For this light momentary affliction is preparing for us an eternal weight of glory beyond all comparison.'

Praising God in Doubt and Pain

Satan would like nothing more than for us to question God's character and benevolence. He uses our broken hearts to goad us into blaming God for our troubles. Praise God that, in His providence, we are supplied with a sure defense against the temptation to deny God's good will.

When we plead with God for relief from pain and don't get what we petition for, we wonder where God has gone. But sometimes we don't see Him in our supplications because He is not there. God does not inhabit our petitions. He is 'enthroned on the praises' of His people (Ps. 22:3).[9]

Are you in pain? Praise Him. Questioning His will? Praise Him. Weary from the dark stains of this world? Praise Him. In your doubt and confusion over your child's struggles, join with the psalmist, who proclaimed,

> I will bless the LORD at all times; his praise shall continually be in my mouth. My soul makes its boast in the LORD; let the humble hear and be glad. Oh, magnify the LORD with me, and let us exalt his name together! I sought the LORD, and he answered me and delivered me from all my fears. (Ps. 34:1-4)

Consider Psalm 22:16-18, where the psalmist sums up his misery with these words:

> For dogs encompass me; a company of evildoers encircles me; they have pierced my hands and feet – I can count all my bones – they stare and gloat over me; they divide my garments among them, and for my clothing they cast lots.

This suffering anticipates the unspeakable agony inflicted on God's Chosen. But four verses later, the psalmist remembers God's goodness and exults:

---

9. 'Yet you are holy, enthroned on the praises of Israel.'

I will tell of your name to my brothers; in the midst
of the congregation I will praise you: You who fear
the Lord, praise him! All you offspring of Jacob,
glorify him, and stand in awe of him, all you offspring of Israel! For he has not despised or abhorred
the affliction of the afflicted, and he has not hidden
his face from him, but has heard, when he cried to
him. (Ps. 22:22-24)

Our affliction is not abhorred by God! Our pain, our doubt
and confusion are acknowledged as He attends to the voice of
our prayers (Ps. 66:19).[10] We find comfort in the loving arms
of a good and gracious Father, who hears our cries of lament.
What one truth do we discover over and over again in the
Psalms – composed of far more laments than mere hymns of
praise? 'The Lord is good.'

Faith Shines Brighter in Darkness

Elsewhere in *Knowing God*, Packer writes, '[God's] ultimate
objective is to bring [people] to a state in which they please
Him entirely and praise Him adequately, a state in which He
is all in all to them, and He and they rejoice continually in the
knowledge of each other's love.'[11]

Pain – physical, emotional, mental, and spiritual – is woven
into the fabric of our fallen world. The affliction of childhood
mental illness is surely not light to our fragile bodies or
momentary to our myopic minds. But true, deep, authentic faith
in Jesus Christ shines glorious light, through even the darkest of
circumstances, on a glory and comfort that will never, ever end.

We need not experience life on earth without hope,
even as we are 'surprised at the fiery trial when it comes'

---

10. 'But truly God has listened; he has attended to the voice of my prayer.'
11. J. I. Packer, 'Chapter Nine: God Only Wise,' *Knowing God* (Downers
Grove, IL: InterVarsity Press, 1993), p. 92.

(1 Pet. 4:12),[12] because with Christ there is a sure future without pain. Therefore, we praise God for His glorious grace, and for the free gift He gave us in His dear Son. God can be trusted with our pain, our questions, and our uncertainty. He will never hide His face from a child who runs to Him in praise.

---

12. 'Beloved, do not be surprised at the fiery trial when it comes upon you to test you, as though something strange were happening to you.'

3

Grief

Sarah has four children, all of whom struggle with mental health challenges. Her oldest, at nearly twenty, has been in and out of their home, in trouble with the law, and is struggling to find his way in the world. Sarah expressed her grief at the loss of the motherhood she longed to have: 'How do you go from grief to fighting for joy? There are some days I seem to do well and then days like today that I am a crumbling mess. God is my anchor, but my emotions are so raw so often.'

Sarah's words sound remarkably like the words my brother uttered when he lost his son to addiction, or my friend Elizabeth's after she lost her daughter suddenly to a seizure. Raising a child with mental health issues can lead families to feelings of profound grief akin to that experienced in the physical loss of a child.

I received an email from a woman who was reeling from the challenges she was facing with her mentally ill daughter. She wrote:

> Last week my friend visited who lost her son three years ago. I just wish (God) would do something big and miraculous about (my daughter's situation). But at least our daughters are alive, and there's hope while there's life. I always want to try and go to a positive note, but there's very little to hang that hope on, except what God says about it.

When we were raising Jackie, I can remember feeling a deep sadness because I wanted her to be the child of my mind's eye.

When she was little, my husband would dream of a day when she would graduate from the Christian school our other kids graduated from, and we would smile and thank God for the success He gave us. I dreamed of a healthy girl – healthy in her mind and in her spirit. I longed for a girl who would assimilate into our family and who was relaxed and happy. I wanted her to reciprocate the love we tried to give to her, and to accept the God we so dearly love. I wanted things to be different. But the Lord saw fit not to heal Jackie or to bring the success we yearned for. With every passing year, it became more apparent that our ending would not be a happy one. And so we grieved.

But our grief activated Christ's compassion. In the midst of our feelings of loss, pain, and frustration over something we desperately wanted but couldn't have, we found a comfort that transcended the grief. We threw ourselves into the grace-drenched embrace of our heavenly Father, where the promises of His comfort became manifest.

In his wonderful book *Gentle and Lowly*, Dane Ortlund wrote:

> If you are in Christ, you have a Friend who, in your sorrow, will never lob down a pep talk from heaven. He cannot bear to hold himself at a distance. Nothing can hold him back. His heart is too bound up with yours. Jesus Christ is closer to you today than he was to the sinners and sufferers he spoke with and touched in his earthly ministry.[1]

The God of All Comfort

A few years ago, my little granddaughter was unhappy about a decision her mother had made. She raged and she questioned; she cried and lamented. But ultimately, through her anger and confusion, she threw herself into her mother's arms for comfort.

---

1. Dane C. Ortlund, *Gentle and Lowly: The Heart of Christ for Sinners and Sufferers* (Wheaton, IL: Crossway Books, 2021), p. 50.

The person who afflicted her was also her source of peace. It is the same for us when we grieve over our children. We rage and question. We are confused and devastated, afflicted by something that God has allowed to happen. But through it all, running into His arms is the only real source of comfort and peace.

The mind of the Lord is vast, His will is sovereign, and even in the midst of unspeakable loss and disappointment, He is supremely good. Through the ages, God's people have leaned into Him in their affliction and grief. Followers of Christ know there is no better place to be than in the safe arms of God. We know that 'the LORD is near to the brokenhearted and saves the crushed in spirit' (Ps. 34:18). We never doubt that God is the 'God of all comfort, who comforts us in all our afflictions, so that we may be able to comfort those who are in any affliction, with the comfort with which we ourselves are comforted by God' (2 Cor. 1:3-4). We trust that God 'heals the brokenhearted and binds up their wounds' (Ps. 147:3). We remember that Jesus said, 'Blessed are those who mourn, for they shall be comforted' (Matt. 5:4). So we do not 'grieve as others do who have no hope' (1 Thess. 4:13). Christians understand that Jesus 'has borne our griefs and carried our sorrows' (Isa. 53:4). And, we are comforted knowing that in His sorrow for His people, 'Jesus wept' (John 11:35).

Elsewhere in *Gentle and Lowly,* Dane Ortlund wrote:

> Our tendency is to feel intuitively that the more difficult life gets, the more alone we are. As we sink further into pain, we sink further into felt isolation. The Bible corrects us. Our pain never outstrips what he himself shares in. We are never alone. That sorrow that feels so isolating, so unique, was endured by him in the past and is now shouldered by him in the present.[2]

---

2. Dane C. Ortlund, *Gentle and Lowly: The Heart of Christ for Sinners and Sufferers* (Wheaton, IL: Crossway Books, 2021), p. 48.

God keeps count of every tear we shed over our afflicted children, and puts them in a bottle. Those tears are kept in His book until the time when He calls us home (Ps. 56:8).[3] We cannot imagine it, because 'no eye has seen, nor ear heard, nor the heart of man imagined, what God has prepared for those who love him' (1 Cor. 2:9). And we wait in God's strong arms of comfort for the day when the dark night of grief will be no more (Rev. 22:5).[4]

Grief and the Goodness of God

Is God only good when the outcome doesn't rip you apart? Can we come to the conclusion that a good God would allow bad things to happen? When our child is ravaged by anxiety, anger, or rigid or illogical thinking, can God's goodness be proclaimed, even as we grieve?

It seems impossible to reconcile the seemingly conflicting promises in the Bible. How do we process the tension between, for example, Psalm 34:19, 'Many are the afflictions of the righteous, but the Lord delivers him out of them all,' and the story of Job? We are promised miracles and tragedies. Sickness and health. Strife and peace. On our own, it is impossible to understand these dichotomies, let alone trust in God's goodness.

But trust comes from seeking out who God is. Because when we seek, we find. And when we find, we see that the tragedies in our lives are not part of God's original good plan for His creation. They come from the human rejection of it. When we seek, we find His sovereignty, His mercy, His grace and, yes, His infinite goodness in making a way for the fallen world to get right with Him.

---

3. 'You have kept count of my tossings; put my tears in your bottle. Are they not in your book?'

4. 'And night will be no more. They will need no light of lamp or sun, for the Lord God will be their light, and they will reign forever and ever.'

It is true the journey to Him can be long and fraught, and maybe there will not be one single miracle on that road. But what God offers through Jesus Christ is hope at the end of the road. Not a wishful thinking kind of hope, but a sure hope – a solid promise of eternal happiness, peace, justice, and an eternity free from pain and strife. And, best of all, a complete, intimate, unhindered relationship with the triune God, in fellowship with Him and every single person who ever wrestled with God and concluded that He is good, and that He is the only way to overcome the rottenness of this world.

The truth is God is good. Every moment. In every outcome. For every human who ever lived, and throughout all eternity. But the weight of the statement, often thrown about in well-meaning triteness, is crushing. We don't see a child held hostage to his emotions as good, nor should we.

A Christian who has come to the conclusion that God is good has not done so easily. We come to it through sweat, tears, and wrestling. Losing a child, in any circumstance, is brutal. As my good friend described it, 'the finality is oppressive.' Like Jacob, those of us who have walked this road will walk it with a limp for the rest of our lives after wrestling with the God we struggle to trust (Gen. 32:25).[5] But through the struggle, with a broken heart, we must proclaim the absolute goodness of the God we have come to know and love. When my brother lost his son to addiction, he told me, 'I believed in Christ before this happened. I must live what I say I believe now.'

If the Creator of the universe is not good, everything falls into hopelessness and despair. Apart from Jesus Christ, there is nowhere else to turn (John 6:68).[6] The ever-present and pervasive pain that characterizes life on earth

---

5. 'When the man saw that he did not prevail against Jacob, he touched his hip socket, and Jacob's hip was put out of joint as he wrestled with him.'

6. 'Simon Peter answered him, "Lord, to whom shall we go? You have the words of eternal life."'

notwithstanding, no answer apart from the Bible offers a more plausible explanation for all that we see, good or bad. Tragedies like losing a child to mental illness, along with victories experienced in some families, are both promised by God. Neither outcome amplifies or diminishes His goodness. The same goodness that heals an afflicted child also keeps another in affliction. This is a hard teaching. Because losing a child, whether physically or to mental illness, is the hardest of roads. But when the hard road meets the hard teaching, the gospel is able to prevail. And when the gospel prevails, there is comfort for those who grieve.

Evil is responsible for Jackie's illness. But what the enemy meant for evil, God will use for good (Gen. 50:20).[7] The statement is no banal platitude. It is a hard-fought truth that is proclaimed after much suffering. God is one hundred percent good. Infinitely, supremely, profoundly, and eternally, in every fiber of His Supreme Being.

As I grieve for my daughter, in my sorrow and through helpless concern for her, I will, after wrestling long, proclaim with the psalmist, 'The Lord is good to all, and his mercy is over all that he has made' (Ps. 145:9). I can conclude nothing else.

The Ultimate Answer to Prayer

In the years since our daughter left, God has graciously shown us that the thing we asked Him to grant – success with Jackie – wasn't ultimate. The ultimate answer to our prayers was God Himself. In His kindness and love, He gave Himself freely and abundantly. When counseling sessions loomed or police lights flashed outside the front door, we knew our weakness and His faithfulness in a way we'd never known them before. Over time, He has enabled us to see that our consummate desire, our highest request, the objective of our seeking, the only door to

---

7. 'As for you, you meant evil against me, but God meant it for good, to bring it about that many people should be kept alive, as they are today.'

eternal life, is delight in the Father through His Son and the fellowship we enjoy with His Spirit.

It is good and right to ask God to provide needs and wants, and to search for answers when we are confused by His actions and grieving deep loss. But ultimately, our prayers must be for His glory and His will. All other prayers – for provision and healing and safety and peace – must remain subordinate to the desire for God Himself. Whatever our circumstances, the Spirit enables us to know God better, rejoice in His plans, love what He loves, and delight in fellowship with Him. Understanding that our ultimate good is knowing and enjoying God keeps us from debilitating disappointment and doubt when we grieve.

We love our daughter. And we trust that God is working for good in her life and in ours, no matter what the end of our story may be. We continue to pray and hope that Jackie, like the prodigal, will return and receive the love and benefit of belonging in our family. But though currently the answer to that prayer remains a 'no,' we're grateful for the sweet comfort we have come to know from our gracious and loving Savior.

4

Guilt and Shame

I am a recovering reacter. Unbridled, I tend to shoot first and ask questions later. God has graciously reined me in over the years, but there are many memories of bombast and overreaction with my children that prick my heart with guilt.

For instance, when my son was fourteen, he had long hair. One summer, after chiding him for the bazillionth time to get his hair out of his eyes, worrying that the perpetual head flick would become permanent, I ordained a haircut. His pleas to promise to manage his bangs were drowned out by my insistence that he be helped along by cutting some of them off. The result was a combination of Amish vogue and Dutch Boy paint can. His look of reproach and panic from the barber chair pressed down on me and guilt flooded my heart. My assurances that the hair would grow back did little to assuage his despair and my regret.

The car ride home was emphatically silent, and looking in the rear view mirror at my sulking little Dutch Boy enveloped me in guilt. My pride had overtaken my acceptance of my son, and threatened to tarnish our relationship. When I insisted on Michael's hair being cut, it was because I was afraid of my own image as a parent and I paid no regard to my son's sense of independence and style. So I sought his forgiveness. I laid out my reasons for wanting his hair cut, and repented my pride and pettiness. My sweet son forgave me, but after nearly twenty years, I haven't lived it down.

Guilt and Shame

One of the prevailing emotions that raising a child suffering from mental illness evokes is guilt. Parenting typical children is hard enough. Parenting a child who is perpetually anxious, or oppositional, or rigid in his thinking, or aggressive takes hard to another level.

When I look back on raising my children, not just Jackie, I can have a propensity to spiral into the darkness of self-reproach and remorse. No matter how much I hear people tell me I am a good mom, the guilt of my mistakes threatens to overshadow any good I have done as a parent. In the case of my son's scruffy mane, his hair grew back and no harm was done. Recovering from missteps in handling the emotions and complexities of mental illness is not as simple. Living in the missed possibilities of hindsight can elicit deep feelings of shame or regret. I admit with great compunction my propensity to have on more than one occasion waxed bombastic in response to Jackie's misdeeds and insubordination. Countless were the times I looked back on an altercation and lamented my behavior, listing the myriad positive alternatives to the response I chose in the moment. I imagined I could feel God's pursed lips and rolled eyes at my umpteenth prayer of repentance over sinning in my anger.

More than the guilt over the occasional (OK, frequent) mishandling of conflict was guilt over how I *felt* about my daughter in those times. If I was being honest on any given day during the darkest times of raising her, my unbridled sentiment was dislike, followed by deep contrition. Soon after Jackie left our home, I emailed a friend:

> I feel so guilty about how I feel. There is no part of me that misses her. None. In fact, the other day she texted out of the blue (on a phone bought for her by a forty-year-old predator), and I couldn't bring myself to respond. I want so much to want to reach out to her. Her attachment issues are so deep that I have been a mother in name only.

I am not bitter. I don't hate her. I just don't want to do it anymore. And I am just so glad that God can handle the way I feel. I know it's wrong. It feels weak.

After corresponding with other families walking this road, I know I was not alone in my feelings. One mother admitted, 'The chaos you describe is exactly what we lived, too. Most days, I wish we had never [adopted our daughter]. Then I feel bad because I know God's hand was over all of us from the first thought of adoption to the many wonderful things that happened along the adoption process.' Another mother wrote, 'I have asked God so many times in the past year, "Why did you call me to love these children?" I am too ashamed to type out some of my other honest prayers!'

Seeking Forgiveness

On the night before we officially adopted Jackie, I heard the dog whimpering from Jackie's bedroom. I burst through the door to discover Jackie squeezing the poor dog mercilessly and yanking her fur in great fistfuls. My reaction was, well, large. Tearing the yowling dog from Jackie, I bellowed a histrionic lecture and stormed from the room to report to my husband, Jackie scuffling tearfully at my heels. After calmly regarding me for several moments, my husband pulled a yowling Jackie onto his lap, gently reminding me that she was most likely terrified at the prospect of making the adoption final. She hadn't meant to hurt the dog. She was just responding to her fear of taking this momentous final step away from her biological family.

Shame sheathed me like tar and feathers. As Steve cradled Jackie in his arms, I knelt beside them, rubbing Jackie's back and whispering apologies for my lack of insight. A few snuggles and prayers of repentance later (me to Jackie and Jackie to the dog) and all was well. But the guilt lingered as a thorn in my side.

Seeking forgiveness is powerful, though complicated, because often, the infractions a child commits that draw the missteps in the first place are brought on by the child. The initial fault is theirs. In other words, they started it. But seeking forgiveness is a potent and effective way to model the grace of the gospel for your child. Acknowledging your own guilt in a conflict and repenting of it before Christ and your child not only pleases the Lord, but disarms the conflict and restores the relationship.

It is important to note that repentance does not equal pandering. True repentance is demonstrating great strength and humility while retaining authority. What better way to ensure safety, love, and care to a child than to admit when you sin against him, then follow up with assurance that your love for him is intact. In God's economy, seeking forgiveness is strength, not weakness.

Breaking the Power of Guilt

Had God not been overseeing every detail of my life and parenting, I would have been crushed under the weight of guilt's condemnation. Even now, years after my children are grown, I fight regret and the frustration over the wisdom of hindsight. But I know, because of Christ's work on the cross, those thoughts are a waste of time, a form of pride that is antithetical to my adoption into the family of God.

Jon Bloom, in an article for *Desiring God* wrote:

> Because sin is alive in our bodies (Rom. 7:23) and because we are beset with weakness (Heb. 5:2), the kind of shame we often experience is a potent combination of failure and pride. We fail morally (sin), we fail due to our limitations (weakness), and we fail because the creation is subject to futility and doesn't work right (Rom. 8:20). We also fail to live up to other people's expectations. And because we are full of sinful pride, we are ashamed of our failures and weaknesses, and will go to almost any length to hide

them from others. This means pride-fueled shame can wield great power over us. It controls significant parts of our lives and consumes precious energy and time in avoiding exposure.[1]

The key to breaking the power of guilt, even the guilt over momentous parenting failures, is what John Piper calls 'gutsy guilt.' This guilt is a combination of fully agreeing that you are guilty and fully knowing God will forgive. And not only forgive but also comfort and assure. No eye rolling. No lip pursing. No condemnation. Just exaltation and love. John Piper points to Micah 7:8-9 in his definition of 'gutsy guilt':

> Rejoice not over me, O my enemy; when I fall I shall rise; when I sit in darkness, the Lord will be a light to me. I will bear the indignation of the Lord because I have sinned against him, until he pleads my cause and executes judgment for me. He will bring me out to the light; I shall look upon his vindication.

Gutsy guilt is confessing our iniquity, agreeing that we deserve punishment, and audaciously and confidently expecting God to forgive. Because He promised He would. John Piper explains further:

> God is both angry with me and he is interceding for me. I love the gospel. I love the grace of God. I love the cross of Jesus. I love to fight for joy as a justified sinner. I hope you sense the sweet sufficiency of the blood and righteousness of Christ, like granite under your feet as all the darkness beats against your life so that you can say, 'rejoice not over me, devil.' When I fall I will rise. Because God is on my side.[2]

---

1. Jon Bloom, 'Breaking the Power of Shame,' *Desiring God* (June 30, 2022). desiringgod.org/articles/breaking-the-power-of-shame

2. John Piper, 'When I Don't Desire God (Part 4),' *Desiring God* (August 19, 2005). desiringgod.org/messages/when-i-dont-desire-god-part-4

Assurance

Guilt is powerful, but God's promises are more so. No matter what we feel or think about ourselves, our failures, and missteps with our children, God's promises apply.

> By this we shall know that we are of the truth and reassure our heart before him; for whenever our heart condemns us, God is greater than our heart, and he knows everything. Beloved, if our heart does not condemn us, we have confidence before God. (1 John 3:19-21)

> Strengthen the weak hands, and make firm the feeble knees. Say to those who have an anxious heart, 'Be strong; fear not! Behold, your God will come with vengeance, with the recompense of God. He will come and save you.' Then the eyes of the blind shall be opened and the ears of the deaf unstopped; then shall the lame man leap like a deer, and the tongue of the mute sing for joy. For waters break forth in the wilderness, and streams in the desert. (Isa. 35:3-6)

> The LORD redeems the life of his servants; none of those who take refuge in him will be condemned. (Ps. 34:22)

> There is therefore now no condemnation for those who are in Christ Jesus. (Rom. 8:1)

> The LORD is good, a stronghold in the day of trouble; he knows those who take refuge in him. (Nahum 1:7)

Jon Bloom continued:

> And there is only one place to hide that offers the protection we seek, where all our shame is covered and

we no longer need to fear: the refuge of Jesus Christ (Heb. 6:18-20). Jesus's death and resurrection is the only remedy for the shame we feel over our grievous sin-failures (Heb. 9:26). There is nowhere else to go with our sin; there is no other atonement (Acts 4:12). But if we hide in Jesus, he provides us a complete cleansing (1 John 1:9). And when that happens, all God's promises, which find their yes in Christ (2 Cor. 1:20), become ours if we believe and receive them. And the grace that flows from these promises to us through faith is all-sufficient and abounding and provides for all our other shameful weaknesses and failures (2 Cor. 9:8). The key to breaking the power of pride-fueled shame is the superior power of humility-fueled faith in the work of Christ and the promises of Christ. Shame pronounces us guilty and deficient. Jesus pronounces us guiltless and promises that his grace will be sufficient for us in all our weaknesses (2 Cor. 12:9-10). Christ is all (Col. 3:11). As we trust Jesus as our righteousness (Phil. 3:9) and our provider of everything we need (Phil. 4:19), shame will lose its power over us.[3]

In my most regrettable moments with Jackie, and even in my memories of them, I have been tempted to forget who I am and who I belong to. God, the ever faithful author of my salvation, calls me to Himself, and teaches me with a loving hand. He urges me toward Scripture, places a trusted friend in just the right place, or plays a song on the radio seemingly just for me. Then I remember without a doubt that He, God the Father, Christ the Redeemer, the Spirit my Counselor, is there to offer forgiveness, wash me in grace, and promise me that, though I am guilty, He is not pursing His lips or rolling His eyes. I am His child, dearly loved, far removed from His wrath and

---

3. Jon Bloom, 'Breaking the Power of Shame,' *Desiring God* (June 30, 2022). desiringgod.org/articles/breaking-the-power-of-shame

condemnation, and ultimately judged guiltless before Him. What a beautiful paradox, to be declared guilty and sentenced to eternal life in the arms of the judge who righteously declared my guilt. Because of Christ's work on the cross, my judge is also my advocate and friend.

5

Fear

Many years ago, I taught a little boy who was stricken with the most severe case of mental illness I had ever encountered or have encountered since. I'll call him Kenneth. Kenneth came to me in first grade. My heart ached when I read his file, and I wondered if I could make a difference with this boy. Though, according to his IQ test he was quite bright, he had a severe learning disability, which was a source of constant frustration for him. He was hyperactive, hostile, and extremely aggressive toward adults and children. He had begun medication at age four to control his hyperactivity, depression, and aggression. His grandparents had been very instrumental in helping him to receive the best care possible, and at age six he had already been hospitalized twice for his behavior. It was also reported that he had a tendency to be cruel to animals, torturing the family cat and attempting to kill birds in their yard. He had occasionally verbally threatened his grandmother, as well. I wondered how such a small child could have gotten so sick. His grandmother provided the answer to that question.

According to Kenneth's grandmother, Kenneth's mother had used cocaine and heroin during her pregnancy with him. His mother raised him until he was three, during which time she lived with various men and sometimes prostituted herself. Kenneth was sexually abused as a toddler by at least one of her clients. His mother finally abandoned him and he went to live with his grandparents. Though his grandparents were loving and cared for him well, the damage was so cataclysmic that their efforts and interventions failed to bring their precious little grandson out of the mire of his condition.

In school, Kenneth was unpredictable from the start. A day without incident was rare. Extraordinarily hyper and dangerously volatile, he would explode without warning, toppling chairs and desks, dumping blocks and Legos on the floor, and terrorizing the other children. His tirades were accompanied by foul commentaries and sophisticated personal affronts against anyone, child or adult, who stood in his way or dared to oppose him. African American children were especially at risk as targets, and he regularly declared his white supremacy, spouting racial slurs and threatening violence. Nearly every day he was sent back from his inclusion classes for anything from squirting glue on students and furniture in art class to sexually harassing his classmates. It had never occurred to me that a first grader could engage in sexual harassment, but the perspicuity of his vulgarity and lewdness left no other way to describe it. Ultimately, we were forced to ban Kenneth from all inclusion classes for the safety of the other children and the sanity of the teachers. After that, he actually seemed to calm down. Apparently, the stress of the inclusion classes caused him to act out, and he seemed to feel more comfortable knowing he would not have to endure the anxiety that accompanied his leaving our classroom.

I spent three years teaching and trying to reach Kenneth, but in the end I was unable to bring about much change. The trauma and abandonment in his life proved too much for him, and he was eventually placed in a residential facility where he would spend the rest of his childhood.

Soon after Kenneth left us, I came across an audiotape used to record some creative stories he had been writing. He would dictate the stories on the tape, and I would type them up for him to illustrate. As I turned on the tape recorder, Kenneth's voice came through in a low, chilling tone. Just above a whisper, Kenneth described in great detail my grizzly murder. He calmly and methodically depicted how he would mutilate, then kill me, relating in detail each weapon and instrument that would be used. He ended the brutal manifesto by saying that the entire episode would be documented on videotape. When Kenneth left my class, he was nine years old.

I kept in contact with his grandmother for the next year or so. Just before Kenneth was remanded to the residential facility, his grandmother had taken to locking her bedroom door at night, because she had awoken one morning to find a hammer by her bed. Kenneth had not remembered placing it there. In fact, during the preceding months he had had several disturbing episodes after which he had no recollection. His grandparents lived in a perpetual state of fear.

Living in Fear

It is natural for parents to feel a certain level of concern and even fear for their children. Raising a child who is afflicted with mental illness casts layers onto that fear. Not only are parents walking this road fearful *for* their child, but they may also be in fear *of* their child because of violence or destructive behavior.

Indeed, there were a few times when I was fearful that Jackie would become aggressive to the point that I could not contain her, especially when my husband was not at home. I feared that the episodes would escalate even more, and that our lives would be upended forever. I feared reputation-ruining false accusations and the potential for social-service investigations. But my pervading fear was largely *for* Jackie, not *of* her. I feared for her future. I feared the uncertainty of how to discipline her and maneuver around her volatility without adding to the trauma that gripped her heart. I feared that she would go the way of her biological parents, lost to addiction. I even feared my own reactions toward her behavior. And I feared failure.

If you are raising a child who is in the throes of mental illness, you may be able to relate to the perennial fear that accompanies it. Peace is elusive. Each morning brings fresh worry because each day is an exercise in the unexpected. I can remember praying daily, 'Lord, please give me a willing heart and a calm stomach.' Butterflies persisted, becoming part of my daily existence.

But God was ever faithful. The countermeasure to the fear was being in constant prayer and remembering to cultivate a habit of meditating on targeted Scriptures. In God's Word, I was reminded that God has given His children a spirit of power (2 Tim. 1:7),[1] and that, like Peter sinking in the waves (Matt. 14:30-31),[2] our focus must be on Christ as we reach to Him for rescue. On my worst days, I visualized Christ reaching out to me as I sank in the waves, pulling me into His strong arms, and offering me assurance. A supernatural comfort would wash over me. In those moments, Christ's love was tangible and I was helped.

Walk the Tightrope

Fear is a deeply unpleasant, deeply human response. In the Bible, the command to 'not fear' applies to a myriad of situations: armies advancing, trials pressing, authorities arresting, angels appearing, and even Jesus materializing. When the risen Christ suddenly stood in the locked room with the disciples, His first words to them were, 'Peace be with you' (John 20:19). In other words, calm down. There is no need to fear. (This sometimes

---

1. 'For God gave us a spirit not of fear but of power and love and self-control.'

2. 'But when he saw the wind, he was afraid, and beginning to sink he cried out, "Lord, save me." Jesus immediately reached out His hand and took hold of him, saying to him, "O you of little faith, why did you doubt?"'

makes me chuckle. How would you react if Jesus suddenly popped into your living room?)

How do we obey God's command to not fear when the fear overwhelms us? Imagine you have been challenged to walk a tightrope across a section of the Grand Canyon. You would be 1,500 feet in the air, faced with a 1,400-foot walk on a two-inch cable, buffeted by 30-mile-per-hour winds. If you succeed, you are guaranteed financial security for life.

You learn that you would be trained and guided by Nick Wallenda, expert tightrope walker, who has successfully made this and other equally terrifying trips before. You have complete assurance that you will not fall, because Nick will take every precaution to bring you safely to the other side. You decide to trust Nick, because he is trustworthy, and you agree to walk the tightrope.

Do you think for one moment, despite your complete trust in Nick, you will not feel some measure of fear while you are trekking across that cable? Of course you will! But as your trust in the guide grows, your assurance will gradually quiet the fear as you forge ahead with courage and fortitude, completing the challenge and claiming the prize.

But there is more. The Grand Canyon is beautiful. With Nick behind you, and despite the intense butterflies in your stomach, you can look up and enjoy the view through the danger of the task. You can appreciate the vistas, the river far below, the incredibly blue sky, and the stark white of the distending clouds. You might catch sight of an eagle in its nest or witness a Bighorn sheep climbing the craggy cliff face. You would behold wonders you might never have seen had you not taken the challenge of the walk.

Raising Jackie felt a lot like being on that tightrope. I knew God was behind me (and before me), but the intensity of the fear made it difficult to trust Him. However, the joy that trumped that fear and pervaded my soul came with meditating on God's assurance that His grace is truly sufficient for me (2 Cor. 12:9).[3] If we had success with Jackie, if she was never healed, if our ending was a happy one or culminated in tragedy, I still had Him. The emotion of fear finally bowed down to a God-fueled faith. A deep and satisfying peace mingled with and muted the intense feeling of fear, and I was able to walk safely to the other side of whatever trial I faced.

And, because of my grace-fueled faith, I was able to look up and notice the absolute beauty in the prayers of our friends, the kindness of our church family, and the sweet fellowship of Christ as we looked to Him in prayer. Common grace became personal, and the fear, though I still felt it to some degree, dimmed next to God's greatness and immense and peculiar love for me.

Shalom

R. C. Sproul, in a lecture for Ligonier Ministries, said:

> What negative prohibition did Jesus utter more than any other prohibition? The answer, 'Do not fear.' Jesus says it so often we miss the significance of it. I've wondered many times why Jesus did that so often, why He used those words so frequently. And I suspect that it has something to do with His intimate knowledge and understanding of the frailty of our human makeup, because we as a people tend to be fearful. It is fear of the future, more than anything else, that drives anxieties and fears, and worries. Because we don't know how difficult, or painful, or troublesome the problems that we face tomorrow will be. Many of the things that happen to us are worthy of fear, because there are fearful things out there. There are

---

3. 'But he said to me, "My grace is sufficient for you, for my power is made perfect in weakness." Therefore I will boast all the more gladly of my weaknesses, so that the power of Christ may rest upon me.'

painful things that we may experience. And not all of our worries go unrealized. We can remember David saying, 'The thing I feared the most has come upon me.' (But) God gives His grace to us in our hour of need in a way we don't really anticipate. So what this comes down to theologically and spiritually, is a question of the relationship between the future, our fears of the future, and faith. Being outside of fellowship with God is an intense and powerful provocation to fear. We begin to fear life itself because we are not really in fellowship with the author of life and the Lord of all life. God is the God of tomorrow.[4]

Jesus promised peace (John 14:27) in the face of trial.[5] This peace is not some fragile, temporary peace. The Hebrews understood it as Shalom, a complete, whole, sound, and tranquil peace. This peace with God is a settled, reconciled, and permanent state of amity with God. It is a finished work that cannot be undone. This is why on the cross, Jesus, before giving up His life, says, 'It is finished' (John 19:30). Jesus accomplished it, apart from anything we have done, because He loves us. Read John 3:16 with fresh eyes: 'For God so loved the world that he gave his one and only Son, that whoever believes in him shall not perish but have eternal life.'

Just because we feel some measure of fear does not mean we have no faith. It just means that our faith isn't perfect yet. Our temporal flesh is broken and weak, and God knows that. That's why He gave us that spirit of power and love and self-control. As we look to God in faith, His Spirit gives us strength to act from an eternal perspective and to resist cowering in our temporal frailty.

---

4. R. C. Sproul, 'How to Deal with Anxiety by R. C. Sproul from Dealing with Difficult Problems' (Ligonier Ministries). Accessed August 1, 2022. ligonier.org/learn/series/dealing-with-difficult-problems/how-to-deal-with-anxiety

5. 'Peace I leave with you; my peace I give to you. Not as the world gives do I give to you. Let not your hearts be troubled, neither let them be afraid.'

Of course, there is a fear we must possess, a feeling reminiscent of the knee-knocking fear we'd face while standing on a ribbon of nylon over the Grand Canyon. That is the fear in the presence of a holy God (Ps. 102:15).[6] God means for this awesome fear to feed our souls.

In the face of all our earthly fears, even the intense fear for our children, God intends for us to trust His promise in Joshua 1:9: 'Have I not commanded you? Be strong and courageous. Do not be frightened, and do not be dismayed, for the LORD your God is with you wherever you go.' Though we may feel afraid, we need not let that fear determine how we act. Our God is guiding us on the tightrope, and He Himself will soothe our fears as we take His hand and start walking.

6. 'Nations will fear the name of the LORD, and all the kings of the earth will fear your glory.'

SECTION TWO

God's Sufficiency in the Fallout

6

The Effects of Mental
Illness on Siblings

My husband and I sat in a Ruby Tuesday across the table from Missy and Shawn, a young couple who have three biological children and two adopted daughters, both of whom have varying degrees of mental illness. The couple were careworn and thrilled to be 'out' without their kids. The evening was relaxed and the conversation filled with stories about our daughters that brought laughter and knowing and affirming nods. But Missy and Shawn's laughter was tinged with weariness and frustration. Their road was hard, and they were burdened for their three healthy children, who were struggling to cope with their sisters' mental illness. 'It's just so nice to be able to talk with someone who can relate!' Missy cried.

Missy and Shawn's oldest child was eleven, and had been a part of their family for nine years. The similarities between their little girl and our daughter were striking. Our hearts ached with anxiety and compassion as we quietly listened to the stories of daily life in their home. The couple's younger children were struggling under the negative fallout of their oldest sister's continual aggressive and demoralizing behavior, and the inordinate attention she required from their parents. Their younger son had anxiety from his sister's perpetual verbal and physical threats, and at seven he was already showing signs of anger and resentment. The tyranny of mental illness is their norm, and the children have never known a life of peace and safety at home. The situation had become so dire in recent months that the couple were exploring the possibility of placing their oldest daughter in another home or residential facility. Missy and Shawn were in agony over the potential decision they faced between helping the daughter they love, and relieving their other children whose lives were upended because of her.

Effects on Siblings

Not surprisingly, childhood mental illness affects the entire family. Because a child in crisis requires so much attention and care, meeting the needs of the other children in the home is challenging. Depending on their age and personality, children respond to the stress and uncertainty of living with an emotionally unstable sibling in varying ways. Some children may act out in order to gain attention. Their parents' gaze always seems to be fixed on their sibling, so they copy the behaviors in the hope of shifting that gaze onto themselves. This often brings ire from their parents instead of the desired positive attention, which may compound their loneliness and frustration. Other children may go in the opposite direction, trying extra hard to 'be good' in an attempt to avoid adding to the heap of their parents' worries. One subject of a study of well siblings of mentally ill children reported, 'I became a perfect child to spare my parents more grief.'[1] Still others may retreat inward, close up emotionally, or sink into anger, resentment, or even a kind of guilt that's akin to survivor's guilt.

Our older daughter, Claire, was in the anger and resentment camp. Even today, at twenty-nine, though she is married, emotionally healthy, and raising four beautiful children, she still struggles with resentment. Jackie came into our lives when Claire was fourteen, and suddenly, not only had Claire

---

1. Laura Jacinto, 'Stuck in the Sibling Relationship: Growing up with a Sibling with a Serious Mental Illness and How Intimate Relationships Later in Life May Be Affected' (ScholarWorks, Smith College, 2009). scholarworks. smith.edu/cgi

become a 'middle child,' she had been thrust into the role of older sister to a little girl who constantly broke or pilfered her things, targeted her mercilessly, and, in her mind (and often in reality), hijacked her parents' attention and affection. Claire responded to the strain and intensity of the day to day with catharsis, often garnering a negative response from us, which only proved to perpetuate her frustration. I can recall feeling guilty that Claire frequently seemed to pull the short straw. In raw moments, and there were plenty of those, I had to take great care not to show resentment toward her for adding to the chaos. I sometimes found myself expecting more from her because she was healthy, and sometimes neglected to consider how she may be feeling. My husband and I were often emotionally depleted, and sometimes it felt nearly impossible to meet Claire's needs. Claire sensed this, which also fed into her resentment toward her sister.

What Do You Want Me to Do For You?

Recently I asked Claire what, if anything, had been helpful for her during the time we were raising Jackie. I wish I would have asked her that more when we were in the midst of the trial. Sometimes, in the thick of raising our children, expediency dictates more than wisdom does. But, oftentimes, children are comforted simply by the mere acknowledgment of a need. Of course it is not possible to meet all their emotional needs, at least not immediately. But simply affirming a need can sometimes be enough to assuage negative emotions and to stave off loneliness.

Sometimes when children act out, they are reacting to an inexpressible, unmet need. Retreating to a bedroom. Slamming a door. Hitting a sibling. Lashing out or crying for what, on the surface, seems to be no reason. Any change in behavior may indicate a felt need they are helpless to articulate. Proactively probing children with questions about their felt needs can preempt potential crises. This takes vigilance and compassion, but there is great value in taking time to read the climate of your child's heart.

Jesus was the master of pointed questions that got at the needs of His followers. In Matthew 20, Jesus was confronted with two men who had a need. Both blind, they were clamoring for His attention in such a way that annoyed the crowd, who rebuked them. But instead of walking by, Jesus turned and asked with compassion, 'What do you want me to do for you?' (Matt. 20:32). I would imagine profound hope and joy welled up in those men's hearts even before Jesus healed them, just for having been acknowledged and treated like someone with worth. Jesus affirmed their need before He met it. And then they followed Him.

Quality Time

On any given day when we were raising Jackie, our calendar was replete with counseling appointments, family therapy sessions, and medical specialist consultations, in addition to normal kid stuff, like soccer games and ballet lessons. This, among the activities my other two children were involved in, all beckoning and jostling for our attention. My husband and I often felt like we were split into many pieces, each piece clamoring for priority. In the free spaces of our calendar, life at home was filled with lie detecting, stolen item finding, temper tantrums, or long and exhausting verbal de-escalations, in addition to run-of-the-mill kid stuff, like homework help, book reading, devotion time, and tuck-ins. I can remember knowing Claire needed more of my attention, but many times could do nothing about it. We had to work hard at being intentional about giving Claire the exclusive time she needed and longed for.

I do realize that our experience involved meeting the needs of one teenager. If your family is more similar to Missy and Shawn's, the challenges to afford each of your children exclusive time cannot be understated. Add mental and physical exhaustion to the lack of time, and the task seems insurmountable. But God longs for you to reach out from the valley, to grab His hand, and to allow Him to turn that insurmountable task into sure hope as you work to meet the needs of your children, leaning on Christ for strength. And remember, '[God] who calls you is faithful; he will surely do it' (1 Thess. 5:24).

El Roi

Even if every effort is made to assure children they are loved and valued, the massive amount of attention and energy a child with mental illness requires from parents can sometimes lead siblings to feel invisible. When children are feeling alone, sometimes simply knowing they are seen and heard is enough to bring comfort and affirmation. Knowing that those who care for them really do see into their heart without judgment or scrutiny can act as a balm to their loneliness.

When a child feels invisible or cast aside, it is good to remind them that the God your family serves is El Roi, 'the God who sees.' Remember Hagar? She was the servant of Sarai (later Sarah) who was given to Abram (later Abraham) to bear him a son, when he and Sarai failed to trust the Lord's promise to give them a child. They took matters into their own hands when Sarai remained barren. Genesis 16:1-6 tells the story.[2]

---

2. 'Now Sarai, Abram's wife, had borne him no children. She had a female Egyptian servant whose name was Hagar. And Sarai said to Abram, "Behold now, the Lord has prevented me from bearing children. Go in to my servant; it may be that I shall obtain children by her." And Abram listened to the voice of Sarai. So, after Abram had lived ten years in the land of Canaan, Sarai, Abram's wife, took Hagar the Egyptian, her servant, and gave her to Abram her husband as a wife. And he went in to Hagar, and she conceived. And when she saw that she had conceived, she looked with contempt on her mistress. And Sarai said to Abram, "May the wrong done to me be on you! I gave my servant to your embrace, and when she saw that she had conceived, she looked on me with contempt. May the Lord judge between you and me!" But Abram said to Sarai, "Behold, your servant is in your power; do to her as you please." Then Sarai dealt harshly with her, and she fled from her.'

Hagar had little control over her circumstances. I would imagine she'd also felt invisible. But in her loneliness and despair, God saw Hagar. This was more than merely locating her whereabouts. Genesis 16:7 records this beautiful statement, 'the angel of the LORD found her.' Scholars say the angel of the Lord is Christ Himself. Jesus sought her out and found her in her despair and loneliness. So in verse 13, Hagar calls God 'El Roi,' which in Hebrew means, 'the God who sees me.' What comfort. What affirmation.

This seeing is a profound knowing. God saw Hagar's plight, her heart, her loneliness, and rejection. And in this seeing, this profound knowing, she was in turn able to see Him: 'Truly here I have seen him who looks after me' (Gen. 16:13). And she was comforted.

Later, in Genesis 21, Hagar was again cast aside, this time with her son Ishmael.[3] Once again, she was rejected and alone, and faced with the certainty that she and her son would die. But once more the Lord found her and, this time, the Bible says, 'God heard' (Gen. 21:17).[4]

God found Hagar. He saw Hagar. He heard her and her son. When your child is feeling alone, remind him, God finds, He sees, and He hears. And assure him that you do, too.

Gospel Expectations

There is a sort of caveat to consider when tending to your children's unique needs. When we were raising our children, I often worried about expecting too much from our mentally healthy kids. But while we sometimes can mistakenly expect too much, it is equally important not to expect too little.

---

3. Genesis 21:10: 'So she said to Abraham, "Cast out this slave woman with her son, for the son of this slave woman shall not be heir with my son Isaac."'

4. 'And God heard the voice of the boy, and the angel of God called to Hagar from heaven and said to her, "What troubles you, Hagar? Fear not, for God has heard the voice of the boy where he is."'

Guilt or pity for a mentally healthy child might lead parents to lower their expectations. Children may think they are being treated unfairly at times and, indeed, that may be true. But the perceived unfair treatment can be an opportunity to show them gospel expectations. Though we were careful not to burden our healthy children with too much responsibility for their sister, we also knew that we could expect more from them because they were healthy in their mind.

One terrible evening, Claire was irate over some personal offense leveled, once again, by her sister. Claire was not even trying to hold her tongue. In earshot of the entire family, including Jackie, she bellowed, 'You should never have adopted her!' Though we acknowledged and even agreed with Claire's anger over whatever it was that Jackie had done, we couldn't allow Claire to sin in that anger. So we disciplined her.

Many circumstances in a mentally well sibling's life are terribly unfair. But sometimes unfair circumstances can foster teachable moments. The gospel doesn't teach fairness, but charity and even self-denial. Gospel solutions can lead to forgiveness, grace, and resiliency, if they are sought with love, validation, and great care. The trials faced by your children have no worldly solution. Only gospel grace and the teachings of Christ will help your mentally healthy children (and your unhealthy ones) thrive and find peace in the situation they are in. Every trial in your home can be an opportunity to point to gospel grace.

When Claire calmed down, we required her to apologize to her sister. In that moment, it was more important for Claire to learn the gospel expectation of forgiving and doing good to her 'enemy' than for her to feel that she had been treated with equity or fairness. Afterwards, when cooler heads prevailed, Claire was able to talk with Jackie, and to express her feelings rationally and even instructively. In turn, Claire received the apology she was due, and was able to offer forgiveness.

Appealing to gospel expectations allowed both girls to give and to receive grace. We were also able to show Claire that the difficult path of forgiveness was sweeter for her heart than the immediate satisfaction of wrath and bitterness.

Jesus' example is a hard teaching. Being the sibling of a mentally ill child is a hard road. When the hard road meets the hard teaching, the gospel is able to prevail in a child's heart.

Leaning on the God of All Comfort

If you are in the midst of the storm, you may be hard-pressed to have enough wherewithal to respond with gospel grace, let alone expect your children to. You are weary, and wrath and bitterness may be all you have in your arsenal. I don't lay claim to long runs of success with our children. Looking back, I wish we would have shown more awareness and compassion toward our healthy daughter. She remembers times of loneliness and helplessness, and feeling as if she had no one to talk to. Her life was in constant turmoil, her father and I were often unavailable, and she sometimes had to go it alone. In fact, this chapter is probably born out of hindsight, which boasts the wisdom of Solomon. But through the successes and failures of those years, God was ever faithful.

The God who sees you is also the God of all comfort, for you and for your children (2 Cor. 1:3).[5] This is the same Lord, don't forget, who made the heavens and the earth, and you, and your child. While you are keeping your calendar, and your commitments, and the well-being of your children, the Lord of all creation is keeping you.

---

5. 'Blessed be the God and Father of our Lord Jesus Christ, the Father of mercies and God of all comfort.'

7

The Effects of Mental Illness on Marriage

Several years ago, I had a student whose adolescence was exacerbating his mental health challenges. He began stealing and vandalizing property, and ultimately was removed from his home because he had begun molesting his younger sister. His mother and I prayed for one another and spoke often, swapping stories and offering each other support. We talked at length about things that worked with our children and things that didn't, as well as the massive weight of emotions that accompanied being in the trenches of childhood mental illness. A common theme in our discussions was the strain our children's illness placed on our marriage. Sometimes as we talked, I could sense bitterness in this women's countenance as she worried over the tension between her and her husband. I was heartbroken to learn a few years later that the couple had gotten a divorce.

Marriage is challenging in the best of circumstances, and raising a child with mental illness compounds those challenges. A mentally ill child's needs are all-consuming, and when regular life responsibilities are thrown in, little or no time may be left for spouses to focus on one another. In our case, to say raising our daughter was a challenge does not begin to describe the countless nights of tantrums and aggression, pervasive deceit, manipulation, stealing, running away, and destructive behavior. And our daughter was a master wedge driver, constantly trying to divide my husband and me. Marriage-crushing stress overran our home, and by the time our daughter left, divorce was an impending cloud threatening to separate us for good.

Protect Your Marriage

In an article for Child Mind Institute, physician Harold S. Koplewicz advises couples who are raising children with psychiatric disorders to set aside time in each day to focus on one another, even if it's as brief as twenty minutes daily. He writes:

> When I see a couple with a very difficult child, I write out on a prescription pad the words 'four hours in a motel.' My clients often laugh, but I tell them I'm serious – and I am. I find it's absolutely crucial for them to take a break from the challenges of parenting and see each other as people. If couples with typically developing children need things like 'date nights' to keep their relationships alive, parents of children who are unusually needy or disruptive need and deserve even more – time to be together without talking about the child.[1]

I wish I could say my husband and I regularly followed this advice, though we did have times when we managed to get away. It was tricky because we were adamant about not burdening our friends and family with our daughter's care. But when things spiraled into darkness, we broke down and took advantage of the love and support of our family and friends, who allowed us to grab some time alone to regroup. That time was precious and essential. On more than one getaway, all we could manage to do was nap, which was just enough to allow us to get back in the game feeling loved and refreshed.

But the respite was temporary, and all too often we found ourselves once again free falling toward discord. Toward the

---

1. Harold S. Koplewicz, 'Don't Let a Child's Disorder Destroy Your Marriage' (Child Mind Institute, Inc., July 23, 2021). childmind.org/article/dont-let-a-childs-disorder-destroy-your-marriage

end of our time raising Jackie, however, my husband became very resolute in rejecting divorce. He told me, 'Raising children is temporary, as hard as it is. But our marriage is forever. We need to make sure we fight for it.' And so we did.

Sinners within the Yoke

Despite the seemingly insurmountable differences my husband and I have encountered in our marriage, even in the darkest days with Jackie, we continued to resolve not to divorce. Often it would have seemed so much easier just to end it and find peace. In the moment, when tensions and emotions were running high, and frustration threatened to undo us, the temptation to split was enticing. What stopped us from making our lives temporally (albeit temporarily) easier by parting ways? In a word: Christ.

Divorcing my husband, apart from the pain it would cause us and our family, would only serve to remove the largest indicator, the brightest illuminator, of my principal sin: pride. Choosing the easy road removes the challenge. The removal of challenge removes the opportunity for growth. A lack of growth causes stagnation in our walk. Stagnation in our walk keeps us from Christ and everything He has for us on this earth. Further, if God used marriage as a type of Christ and His church, should we destroy it for the sake of issues that have nothing to do with salvation and everything to do with our own pride?

God admonishes us in 2 Corinthians 6:14 not 'to be unequally yoked with unbelievers. For what partnership has righteousness with lawlessness? Or what fellowship has light with darkness?' My husband and I are not unequally yoked in our belief in our Lord Jesus Christ. But we are sometimes unequally yoked in disputable matters (Rom. 14).[2] We have more than once almost allowed ourselves to be ripped apart

---

2. Romans 14:1 'Accept the one whose faith is weak, without quarreling over disputable matters' (NIV).

because of opinion. However, we do not get a free pass to unyoke ourselves from each other for this reason alone: we both have submitted to the easy yoke of Christ (Matt. 11:30).[3] We are believers and, as such, we have no right to tear apart what God has joined.

What, then, do we do with our jostling and bumping within the yoke Christ has fitted us with? Christ's yoke is easy in the sense that we can put to rest our confusion and uncertainty about our future in Him. We are saved, secure, and bound to Christ eternally. But we're still here on earth, tilling the rocky, seemingly impassable soil of our marriage. How then, in the face of demoralizing stress, do we learn to walk in step with one another as sinners within the yoke?

The Love Language of Marriage

In my marriage, especially when we were raising Jackie, I have often felt frustrated, hurt, tired, angry, and sometimes unloved. I know my husband has felt the same at times. Although there were other times when my husband and I were galvanized by a particularly difficult incident or season with Jackie, we also had just as many times when we felt isolated and angry. We responded to our feelings about the other person's failing to meet our expectations. He didn't affirm me or a parenting decision I made. I didn't serve him when he was feeling overwhelmed. So we became bitter toward one another. We had corroborated with ourselves instead of denying ourselves. So we were unhappy.

I know what the world's wisdom says about marriage. If I am unhappy, I should leave and find someone who will make me happy. Or I should just 'eat, pray, and love' my way to happiness by pursuing endeavors that would lead me to 'find myself.' Sometimes in the thick of raising Jackie, I felt it would be easier

---

3. 'For my yoke is easy, and my burden is light.'

to make parenting decisions on my own. At least I would only have the stress of the parenting without the stress of the marriage. Of course, those thoughts were steeped in self-absorption, and utterly ignored consideration of Christ or my husband.

Burk Parsons said, 'The love language of all marriages is self-denial.'[4] Christ would have me carry my cross right up to the top of the hill of my marriage, loving my husband with no conditions and through the fiercest of storms. Why? Because my husband is my brother in Christ. He is a fellow believer, who came to Christ in 1997 right alongside me, entering into the covenant of grace, which binds us even more than our covenant of marriage. Christ would have me obey Ephesians 4:31-32, 'Let all bitterness and wrath and anger and clamor and slander be put away from you, along with all malice. Be kind to one another, tenderhearted, forgiving one another, as God in Christ forgave you.' He has told me in John 15:12, 'This is my commandment, that you love one another as I have loved you.' And in Luke 6:31, 'And as you wish that others would do to you, do so to them.' Shouldn't I be considering Colossians 3:12-14?

> Put on then, as God's chosen ones, holy and beloved, compassionate hearts, kindness, humility, meekness, and patience, bearing with one another and, if one has a complaint against another, forgiving each other; as the Lord has forgiven you, so you also must forgive. And above all these put on love, which binds everything together in perfect harmony.

These marvelous commands do not become null and void when a certain threshold of stress is surpassed. The prescription in 1 Corinthians 13 for godly love does not include a caveat for seemingly insurmountable challenges.

---

4. Burk Parsons, 'The Orthodoxy of Community' (Ligonier Ministries, February 25, 2016). ligonier.org/learn/articles/orthodoxy-community

Living the 'Love Passage'

A few summers ago, I typed out the words of 1 Corinthians 13 and now keep them in a frame above my desk. When I am tempted to 'keep a record of wrongs,' I go to these framed words. I pray for God to remind me how much He loves my husband, and how much Christ suffered so I could have a godly marriage, even in the midst of the great challenges of raising our difficult child.

'Love is patient and kind. Love does not envy or boast; it is not arrogant or rude' (1 Cor. 13:4-5). When you are in the trenches of raising a child with mental health challenges, your patience and kindness will be tested. You may be using all of your energy demonstrating these virtues toward your child, with nothing left over for your spouse. I can remember being totally in step with my husband during crises, but lashing out at him with harsh impatience at smaller issues. But your spouse is the very first person you should extend patience and kindness to, especially in the trenches. Our sin nature makes this difficult in the best of circumstances. A life in constant crisis makes it nearly impossible.

John Piper, in an article for *Desiring God,* says this about patience:

> For the Christian, this strength comes from God. That is why Paul (in Col. 1:11) is praying for the Colossians. He is asking God to empower them for the patient endurance that the Christian life requires. But when he says that the strength of patience is 'according to [God's] glorious might,' he doesn't just mean that it takes divine power to make a person patient. He means that faith in this glorious might is the channel through which the power of patience comes. Patience is indeed a fruit of the Holy Spirit (Gal. 5:22), but the Holy Spirit empowers (with all his fruit) through 'hearing with faith' (Gal. 3:5). Therefore, Paul is praying that

God would connect us with the 'glorious might' that empowers patience. And that connection is faith.[5]

Faith in Christ means having faith in His strength and sufficiency to empower you to love the way He prescribes. When I was in the middle of a crisis with Jackie, I admit I could tend to be arrogant because of my experience of working with emotionally disturbed kids. My arrogance, coupled with a lack of patience, brought me low on many occasions. In the moments that I disregarded my husband's input, or snapped at him in frustration, or acted haughtily in my 'superior knowledge,' it was clear I was disconnected from my source of power. Staying connected to God, through His Word and prayer on a daily (sometimes even minute by minute!) basis is vital. Patience, kindness, and humility are impossible apart from Christ (John 15:5).[6]

Love 'does not insist on its own way; it is not irritable or resentful' (1 Cor. 13:5). I never thought of myself as a resentful person. But living in crisis mode had a way of illuminating sins I never even knew I had the potential to commit! It is only with God's strength that I can remember to open my mind to other ideas when I think I know best. Some of our worst nights with Jackie were worsened because of my husband's and my reactions to one another in the midst of the crisis. When we were in our weakest moments, without breaking to seek the Lord, we tended toward irritability and resentment as our default.

In speaking of 1 Corinthians 13, Charles Spurgeon wrote:

> What does this teach us at the outset, but that a
> salvation which leads to [this kind of love] must be of

---

5. John Piper, 'The Power for Our Patience,' *Desiring God* (May 26, 2013). desiringgod.org/articles/the-power-for-our-patience

6. John 15:5: 'I am the vine; you are the branches. Whoever abides in me and I in him, he it is that bears much fruit, for apart from me you can do nothing.'

God, and must be wrought in us by His power? Such a comely grace can never grow out of our fallen nature. If charity (love) be in any man and abound, God must have the glory of it; for assuredly it was never attained by mere natural effort, but must have been bestowed by that same hand which made the heavens. So then, brethren, I shall hope when I conclude to leave upon your minds the impression of your need of the grace of God for the attainment of love. I would not discourage you, but I would have you feel how great a labour lies before you, and how impossible it will be unless you are girt with a strength beyond your own.[7]

In other words, this level of love Paul described is quite impossible outside of God's strength and grace.

'Love bears all things, believes all things, hopes all things, endures all things' (1 Cor. 13:7). We cannot bear anything without God's strength. God-fueled love breeds a divine optimism, a sure hope, and a strength that allows us to bear not only the stress and strain of the day to day in raising our mentally ill children, but also the strength to bear the sin of our spouse when they are disconnected from the power source.

Even now, years after raising our daughter, I am still very far from conquering my relentless regard of self. I still forget, more than I care to admit, to connect to the source of strength that will compel me to live out these verses. But I know that God does not turn away nor do His care and provision rise and fall with my inconsistency. Our yoke is held firm by the One who placed it there.

---

7. Charles H. Spurgeon, '1 Corinthians 13 – Spurgeon's Verse Expositions of the Bible – Bible Commentaries' (StudyLight.org). Accessed August 2, 2022. studylight.org/commentaries

8

Falsely Accused

My husband cried when he read the notice. The word 'perpetrator' leapt from the page, searing into him like a scarlet letter. The word 'victim' sat next to Jackie's name. We were being investigated for child abuse.

Two weeks earlier, on the advice of Jackie's trauma therapist, we had decided to have Jackie evaluated by a child psychiatrist. Jackie's behaviors had become so volatile and bizarre that the counselor felt we needed a more extensive battery of testing.

My husband had taken her to the intake appointment, which was comprised of a thirty-minute interview with Jackie and a ten-minute follow-up conversation with my husband. That was the last time we'd ever allow anyone to speak to our daughter without one of us being present.

Jackie's thirty minutes with the psychiatrist had included some colorful hyperbole, grossly exaggerating our role in altercations in direct proportion to a downplay of her own. Whether he believed Jackie or saw through her embellishments, his role as a mandated reporter dictated a call to social services.

A few days later, without our knowledge or consent, a social worker had visited Jackie's school, the small Christian school where our other children had attended, and interviewed her. Our dear friends at the school had not been allowed to notify us. It was Jackie who called me at work in a torrent of anxiety, telling me through sobs about the lady who came to ask her questions. Jackie realized what she had done when the truth came home that she could be removed from our family. But her regret came too late. The investigation had been opened.

So distraught was my husband that he collapsed onto a chair and wept. One forty-minute visit to a doctor, from whom we were seeking help, was now threatening to derail his reputation as a business owner and to destroy his integrity. I had received my own notice, and had also been named as a perpetrator. I held the paper loosely, staring at my husband in disbelief, envisioning my own reputation and teaching career vanishing in disgrace. We had never felt so betrayed, nor so frightened.

Trusting in What God Has Commissioned

We have spoken to other parents who have experienced similar situations. Missy and Shawn, the young couple whom we were mentoring through the challenges they are facing in their own family, shared with us that their daughter once told her grandmother that Shawn had pulled down her pants and spanked her – while she was having her period! The gory details she fabricated about the alleged incident were so convincing that her grandmother believed her. Shawn was eventually able to set his mother straight, but from that day forward, he abdicated all discipline to Missy. Every subsequent interaction with his daughter is now carefully measured. The fear of the devastating effects one false accusation could bring robbed him of the ability to be the father he longed to be to her, and the one she so desperately needed.

In our culture, long-held practices of natural, consequence-based methods of discipline are regarded as archaic and even cruel, creating the potential to draw the ire of public scrutiny. A child who is emotionally unstable may unwittingly – or wittingly – use your attempts at discipline against you. Yet Christian parents are commissioned by God to raise their children, mentally ill or otherwise, in the 'discipline and instruction of the Lord' (Eph. 6:4).[1] Deciding how to discipline a mentally ill child takes great discernment.

God's Word can be trusted to have the final say in everything we do as parents. While we held to biblical principles of discipline with Jackie, our trust of the Lord needed some serious shoring up in the face of the risk of false accusation and public scrutiny, as well as the fear of adding to the trauma that produced her mental illness in the first place. Indeed, our trust was tested on more than one occasion.

In recent years, the risk of public scrutiny seems to be even greater as our culture moves faster and further from the Judeo-Christian principles that once advised it. Prayer and godly counsel are crucial. The Lord is gracious in His care and guidance. He can be trusted to walk beside you as you cling to Him in obedience and look to Him for wisdom in your efforts to love and shepherd your child.

When we were being investigated for abuse, my mind (and my stomach) churned with intense fear and doubt as I struggled to recount every detail of every conflict we had ever had with Jackie. Yes, we had sometimes spanked her bottom when she was little. Yes, some altercations had become physical when she became aggressive. Yes, there were times when we had to physically restrain her to keep her from harming herself or us, or from destroying the house. In my heart I was certain we had acted appropriately in those situations. Yet I still felt guilty somehow. The mere suggestion that we had abused one of our children was enough to plant seeds of doubt in my mind. I wondered how many of those seeds planted in other people's minds would flourish into their determination of our guilt.

As we waited for the investigation to play out, only the good assurances of God kept us from falling into despair.

---

1. 'Fathers, do not provoke your children to anger, but bring them up in the discipline and instruction of the Lord.'

Ceaseless Prayer

Living in the midst of a false accusation means living in the looming shadow of the unknown. The first and best defense against despair is to 'pray without ceasing' (1 Thess. 5:16). R. C. Sproul wrote, 'My tomorrow and your tomorrows are in the hands of God. We make our requests before Him and we trust our tomorrows to His sovereignty.'[2] Isaiah 26:3 says of God, 'You keep him in perfect peace whose mind is stayed on you.' What clear and beautiful imagery. A deep and satisfying peace overtakes fear when in prayer you 'stay your mind' on Christ.

In addition to personal prayer, reaching out to others for prayer lifts to the Lord more supplication on your behalf. Our church family, my school family, and extended friends and family acted as faithful prayer warriors.

The more specific we are in asking for prayer the better. Are you anxious? Ask for prayers for peace. Are you feeling angry toward your child? Ask for prayers for grace. Are you paralyzed with self-doubt? Ask for prayers for clarity and assurance. The more specific you can be in your requests, the more precise your friends will be able to be in their intercession for you.

Scripture List

Gathering an arsenal of scripture was an effective weapon against the constant barrage of accusations by the enemy. The adversary tried with great gusto to convince us of our guilt. He sowed little seeds of doubt that threatened to blossom into second-guessing. There was just enough truth in those seeds to make us feel we were the worst parents on the planet. He also attempted to coerce us toward hatred and resentment toward Jackie.

Listing scripture served as a reminder to me (and to the enemy) that God made solid, incorruptible promises to His people:

---

2. R. C. Sproul, 'Biblical and Theological,' *The Aquila Report* (January 28, 2018). theaquilareport.com/r-c-sprouls-warning-concerning-prayer-2

Fear not, for I am with you; be not dismayed, for I am your God; I will strengthen you, I will help you, I will uphold you with my righteous right hand. (Isa. 41:10)

Do not be anxious about anything, but in everything by prayer and supplication with thanksgiving let your requests be made known to God. And the peace of God, which surpasses all understanding, will guard your hearts and your minds in Christ Jesus. (Phil. 4:6-7)

When I am afraid, I put my trust in you. (Ps. 56:3)

Be strong and courageous. Do not fear or be in dread of them, for it is the LORD your God who goes with you. He will not leave you or forsake you. (Deut. 31:6)

Casting all your anxieties on him, because he cares for you. (1 Pet. 5:7)

I sought the LORD, and he answered me and delivered me from all my fears. (Ps. 34:4)

Even though I walk through the valley of the shadow of death, I will fear no evil, for you are with me; your rod and your staff, they comfort me. (Ps. 23:4)

Who shall separate us from the love of Christ? Shall tribulation, or distress, or persecution, or famine, or nakedness, or danger, or sword? (Rom. 8:35)

The LORD will fight for you, and you have only to be silent. (Exod. 14:14)

No weapon that is fashioned against you shall succeed, and you shall refute every tongue that

> rises against you in judgment. This is the heritage
> of the servants of the LORD and their vindication
> from me, declares the LORD. (Isa. 54:17)

When the promises of God become your focus, a narrative will form that can serve as a bulwark against the enemy, and act as a fear-quelling balm to your unsettled heart.

Continuing to Love

This may seem a strange reminder. What healthy parent would need to be exhorted to keep loving their children? Yet the intensity of this trial was so great that my husband and I found ourselves struggling against resentment toward Jackie. After all, it was her false accusation that placed us under the scrutiny of the authorities. It was her embellishments that turned our seeking help into being labeled as perpetrators. We kept thinking *we are the victims here,* yet it was our daughter who was regarded as such.

But she needed us. She was in as much pain and carried as much fear as we did. She was burdened with regret and anxiety over the threat of being returned to the system. She was a hurting little girl.

The wars that are waged in the face of childhood mental illness are not waged against your child, but against the illness itself. And, as the Bible teaches, 'against the rulers, against the authorities, against the cosmic powers over this present darkness, against the spiritual forces of evil in the heavenly places' (Eph. 6:12). Our flesh would convince us to be angry at our child. Our Savior would compel us to take to our knees in prayer for her.

My daily prayer during this trial was for Jesus to give me His heart. My own weary heart was wracked with fear and resentment, and could not adequately love Jackie through it. Christ's heart in me could compel me to hug and nurture her when she was anxious, read her stories at tuck-ins, play games with her, and pray with and for her, as He opened my eyes to the real enemy. It did not come naturally, but Jesus was faithful and generous with His own supernatural love.

Christ Can Relate

Jesus knew something about false accusation. The gospels record a frustrating scene near the end of His earthly life.

Betrayed by one of His own, Jesus was brought before the Jewish authorities. These leaders of Israel had been commissioned to keep God's covenant and prepare their people for the coming Messiah. Acting in blind and ignorant jealousy, they launched a campaign to discredit and destroy Christ.

Devoid of any real evidence of wrongdoing, the leaders stirred up false witnesses who twisted Jesus' words and used them against Him. They accused Him of misleading Israel and forbidding people to pay their taxes. They tried to convince the Roman authorities that Jesus would try to destroy the Temple and overthrow Caesar.

Indeed, Jesus did say He was the Lord of a Kingdom and that He would destroy the Temple. But His words were taken out of context and used to fit the Jewish leaders' damning agenda-driven narrative. Jesus had no recourse. An entity with great power and no heart was bearing false witness against Him. The very men who were called and commanded to uphold God's Holy Law were brazenly breaking it.

What was Jesus's response? He told the truth. When the high priest charged Jesus to tell him if He was the Messiah, Jesus replied, 'You have said so. But I tell you, from now on you will see the Son of Man seated at the right hand of Power and coming on the clouds of heaven' (Matt. 26:64).

Jesus's only concern was for His Father's will. He did not defend Himself. He did not seek to set the record straight. He was given a mission by His Father, and He trusted Him to keep

Him in that mission. Jesus looked past the false accusations to the glory that was set before Him. He also knew that those who had ears to hear the truth would hear it and believe Him, even if the blind authorities did not.

Secure in His Hands

A few weeks after the receipt of our letters from social services, the social worker who interviewed Jackie at school visited our home. By God's grace, and to our great relief, we were cleared of all charges. We set about the business of healing, though the veil of fear that we might be one blowup away from another false accusation hung pale and menacing in our home.

Still, what we learned about our great God in the midst of this terrible storm convinced us that even if we had lost our jobs and reputations, God would still be sufficient, Jesus would still be our Savior, and our life would still be secure in His hands. Knowledge of the sovereignty and sufficiency of Christ truly did provide that promised transcending peace.

9

Dredging Up the Past

Not long before Jackie left our home, I began experiencing intense anxiety. The angst would become so profound that it sometimes manifested physically. One evening, during a family trauma therapy session, I suddenly began to tremble to the point that my teeth were chattering. What was the catalyst? The therapist had turned the attention to me, asking me to tell her about my growing up. At the end of the hour, I was exhausted and so tense I could barely function. I struggled to understand what was happening to me. My emotions were unraveling and I felt like I was losing my grip. It was terrifying and unexpected.

During the next session, the trembling returned. The therapist noticed my chattering teeth and asked to see me alone for the next appointment. Probing me further, she began asking me about my family, and ultimately the conversation turned to my mom. My mother had significant mental health issues which went undiagnosed her entire life. But the impact her illness had on our family was profound. I had been in counseling before to deal with the aftermath of the emotional abuse that accompanied my mother's illness, so I thought the issues had been put to rest. Apparently, the effects had lain dormant until confronting Jackie's issues brought them erupting to the surface, pouring forth during those counseling sessions. It was one of the most painful and frightening experiences of my life.

Dredging Up the Past

Very often, children inflicted with mental illness require counseling, which sometimes includes intensive therapy for the whole family. Trauma therapy in particular seeks to mine past events in order to heal current hurts. For some parents, this may mean dredging up their own unresolved past trauma. This can be surprising and devastating, an unintended consequence of trying to get to the bottom of their child's illness.

We all carry some degree of hurt from our childhood. In my case, Jackie's hostility and her propensity to push specific buttons in those around her mirrored some of my mom's behaviors. Like the time my mother threw a TV tray at my father and broke the glass on a picture hanging above the couch. Or her thundering tirades that competed with the whir of the vacuum cleaner on any given Saturday morning. Or the deftly placed guilt trips that held the rest of us hostage to her will. Each day of my childhood brought uncertainty over which version of my mother we would wake up to. Inconsistency was the only constant. So when Jackie was breaking out in hostility toward someone in the family, it would provoke a response that found me fighting the urge to cower in anxiety and fear. It was almost as though I was deeply intimidated by this tiny firecracker of a girl.

I eventually learned the tight chest and intense feelings of disquiet during certain episodes were visceral reactions to past trauma in my own life. I had always prided myself in my emotional strength. I also am super wary of anything that smacks of psychoanalysis. This vulnerability was a hard pill to swallow, but one that was necessary to bring me to a point where I realized the pride was foolish and harmful. Our past shapes who we are today, good or bad, but it doesn't have to condemn or paralyze us.

The Necessity of Remembering

If you're like me, you tend to try to deeply bury past hurts, as if forgetting them will somehow heal the pain they cause. I have learned that this is not so. Not only does suppressing pain keep the wound open, it keeps you from finding out what God means to do with your pain. When the counselor routed out the wounds of my past, I wrestled with God, wondering why He would bring another person into my life who evoked such deep emotional strain. But over time, I realized that the pain I experienced with my mother served me well in trying to help Jackie. When the pain was finally dealt with, it diminished, and my empathy increased. Once again, what the enemy meant for evil, God used for a work of healing in me and the provision of an empathetic ally for Jackie.

John Piper points to Paul as an example of the transformative power of a painful past placed in the hands of God. Before he was confronted by Christ on the Damascus road (Acts 9), Paul was a murderer of God's people.[1] He was implicit in Christ's death, as well. He was the guy standing by holding the coats while the Jews stoned the Apostle Stephen (Acts 7:58)![2] I'm sure Paul held memories of gruesome trauma that stuck with him his whole life. Piper explains:

> Here's something so horrible in Paul's life, in his background, that he never, never stopped taking it into account. He never got beyond it. He never stopped thinking on it and its implications; it never stopped playing an emotional role in his life. So, I'm suggesting that the way forward is not to be sought mainly in forgetting – or, God forbid, minimizing – the horror, but in fact remembering, owning, finding Paul's supernatural way of living with the grief and the

---

1. Acts 9:1-5 'But Saul, still breathing threats and murder against the disciples of the Lord, went to the high priest and asked him for letters to the synagogues at Damascus, so that if he found any belonging to the Way, men or women, he might bring them bound to Jerusalem. Now as he went on his way, he approached Damascus, and suddenly a light from heaven shone around him. And falling to the ground, he heard a voice saying to him, "Saul, Saul, why are you persecuting me?" And he said, "Who are you, Lord?" And He said, "I am Jesus, whom you are persecuting."'

2. 'Then they cast him out of the city and stoned him. And the witnesses laid down their garments at the feet of a young man named Saul.'

wrong that was done, in such a way that it does not paralyze ministry but mysteriously, painfully – even beautifully – deepens it.[3]

Healing is not found in the suppression of painful memories, but in living in them, through them, and with them. C. S. Lewis wrote that 'God whispers to us in our pleasures, speaks in our conscience, but shouts in our pain: it is His megaphone to rouse a deaf world.'[4] In other words, our pain in this fallen world shouts us back to God, where He can use it for good (Rom. 8:28).[5] Piper contends that 'Romans 8:28 is not a promise of escape from misery, but a promise of being kept from delusion and unbelief and destruction in it, and that in due time God works it out for our good.'[6] And also for the good of others (2 Cor. 1:3-4).[7]

All Things New

Jesus Christ is the maker and the re-maker. In John 4, we read a story of a remarkable transformation from a trauma-oppressed woman to a gospel-freed daughter of the Living God. Jesus made a scandalous trip to a region no self-respecting Jew would dare step foot in. He sought out a woman whom He knew to be burdened and maltreated. He began by making an innocuous request, 'Give me a drink' (John 4:7). In reality, the request

---

3. John Piper, 'How Do I Recover from an Unbearable Tragedy?' *Desiring God* (August 28, 2020). desiringgod.org/interviews/how-do-i-recover-from-an-unbearable-tragedy

4. C. S. Lewis, 'Chapter Six: Human Pain,' *Problem of Pain* (Glasgow: Fount Pbs., 1940), p. 91.

5. 'And we know that for those who love God all things work together for good, for those who are called according to his purpose.'

6. John Piper, 'How Do I Recover from an Unbearable Tragedy?' *Desiring God* (August 28, 2020). desiringgod.org/interviews/how-do-i-recover-from-an-unbearable-tragedy

7. 'Blessed be the God and Father of our Lord Jesus Christ, the Father of mercies and God of all comfort, who comforts us in all our affliction, so that we may be able to comfort those who are in any affliction, with the comfort with which we ourselves are comforted by God.'

was anything but innocuous. To speak to a woman in public, let alone a woman from Samaria, was deeply ignominious. 'How is it that you, a Jew, ask for a drink from me, a woman of Samaria?' (For Jews have no dealings with Samaritans.)' (John 4:9). From there, He deftly steered the conversation to the woman's past, tipping His prophetic hand and getting her attention. 'You are right in saying, "I have no husband"; for you have had five husbands, and the one you now have is not your husband' (John 4:18). After compassionately validating her concerns about worship, He explained with great assurance the true nature of it. 'But the hour is coming, and is now here, when the true worshipers will worship the Father in spirit and truth, for the Father is seeking such people to worship him' (John 4:23). Finally, when the woman counters that all things will be made clear after the Messiah comes, He revealed His true identity. 'I who speak to you am he' (John 4:25-26). And she believed Him. 'Come, see a man who told me all that I ever did. Can this be the Christ?' (John 4:29). The past trauma in her life was dredged up and acknowledged, she was accepted and drawn in, and her life was transformed. She became one of the most famous and enthusiastic evangelists of the Bible!

In the 'Woman at the Well,' we see Christ work in the same way He works in us when we are hurting. He seeks us out, draws us in, lavishes on us great love and compassion, and does not condemn us or wag a finger at our past mistakes. Our suffering does not repel Him. He, too, in His earthly life, though without a trace of sin, experienced great rejection, and pain. Dane Ortlund wrote in his book *Gentle and Lowly,* 'It is not only that Jesus can relieve us from our troubles, like a doctor prescribing medicine; it is also that, before any relief comes, he is with us in our troubles, like a doctor who has endured the same disease.'[8]

---

8. Dane C. Ortlund, 'Chapter Four: Able to Sympathize,' *Gentle and Lowly: The Heart of Christ for Sinners and Sufferers* (Wheaton, IL: Crossway Books, 2021), p. 47.

Paul said, in Galatians 2:20, 'I have been crucified with Christ. It is no longer I who live, but Christ who lives in me.' And in 2 Corinthians 5:17, 'Therefore, if anyone is in Christ, he is a new creation. The old has passed away; behold, the new has come.' Through the prophet Isaiah, God declared, 'Remember not the former things, nor consider the things of old. Behold, I am doing a new thing; now it springs forth, do you not perceive it? I will make a way in the wilderness and rivers in the desert' (Isa. 43:18-19). And from His throne, Christ proclaimed, 'Behold, I am making all things new' (Rev. 21:5). But we are still on this old, unredeemed earth, where 'there is nothing new under the sun' (Eccles.1:9). We are still living in the mire of our condition, tilling the rocky soil of our lives, operating under the oppression of our memories. But Jesus is right there with us, a comforter, advocate, and dear friend. He is a counselor and keeper. 'The LORD will keep you from all evil; he will keep your life. The LORD will keep your going out and your coming in from this time forth and forevermore' (Ps. 121:7-8). The author of life died so we could be made new and our pain redeemed and used for His great kingdom purposes.

Burden Free

Consider this scene in John Bunyan's magnum opus, *Pilgrim's Progress*. Thus far in the book, the main character, Christian, has been trudging toward the Celestial City with a great burden on his back. On his journey, he encounters the cross, which releases the burden and compels him to leap with joy in praise:

> Up this way, therefore, did burdened CHRISTIAN run; but not without great difficulty, because of the load on his back. He ran thus till he came at a place somewhat ascending; and upon that place stood a Cross, and a little below, in the bottom, a sepulchre. So

I saw in my dream that just as CHRISTIAN came up to the cross, his burden loosed from off his shoulders, and fell from off his back, and began to tumble; and so continued to do till it came to the mouth of the sepulchre, where it fell in, and I saw it no more. Then was CHRISTIAN glad and lightsome, and said, with a merry heart, 'He hath given me rest by his sorrow, and life by his death.'[9]

For a follower of Jesus Christ, the greatest burden, our sin, is something we no longer have to bear. That alone makes the temporal burdens of life lighter. 'Behold, I have taken your iniquity away from you, and I will clothe you with pure vestments' (Zech. 3:4). Because the shame of our past is literally buried with Christ, we can unreservedly give all our other burdens to the One who has the strength to bear them. What freedom this allows! Without the burden of condemnation, or grief, or anxiety over our past, we are free to attend to the needs of our children with great peace and empathy, assured that God has redeemed our yesterdays and freed us from their hold. We can exult, along with Christian:

> Thus far did I come laden with my sin,
> Nor could aught ease the grief that I was in,
> Till I came hither. What a place is this!
> Must here be the beginning of my bliss!
> Must here the burden fall from off my back!
> Must here the strings that bound it to me crack!
> Blest cross! blest sepulchre! blest rather be
> The Man that there was put to shame for me![10]

---

9. John Bunyan, *Pilgrim's Progress* (Westwood, NJ: Barjour Books, 1985), pp. 35-36.

10. Ibid.

SECTION THREE

Guidance in the Storm

10

Gospel Grace

When Jackie was about twelve years old, just after Christmas, Claire's laptop went missing. Of course, our first inclination was to blame Jackie, who vehemently denied taking it. We turned over every inch of her bedroom, asked the school to be on the lookout for it, and searched her backpack every night. Claire was certain Jackie had taken it, and was furious with us for concluding that she couldn't have. We'd scrutinized every corner of Jackie's bedroom, and found nothing. Still, every night for a week we grilled her and searched her room, always being met with incredulous and convincing denials and a fruitless search.

After about a week, when Claire was searching her own bedroom once again, the computer suddenly materialized under a chair cushion in the corner of her room. The history had been deleted. Jackie had, indeed, taken the computer and, sensing that it would only be a matter of time until we caught up to her, covertly returned the laptop to Claire's room, hoping that Claire would just think she'd misplaced it under the cushion.

I was furious. I laid into Jackie, assaulting her with a ranting lecture. Looking back, I regret not simmering down before confronting her, but the stress of the week and the fact that we were so audaciously deceived brought me to my boiling point. I am afraid I sinned in my anger that night.

After some minutes of angry berating and tears, Jackie's, Claire's, and mine, Claire and I retreated downstairs to cool off, while Steve took Jackie into our room and began gently talking with her. At this point, Jackie was showing signs of genuine contrition, explaining that she had wanted to own up to stealing the computer, but it had gotten to the point where she was in so deep she couldn't get herself out. In the end, she'd decided to return it and hoped Claire would chalk it up to oversight. I'm not sure we had ever been this irate over her actions, and I think it worried her.

After several minutes, my husband called Claire upstairs. During his gentle decompression, he had begun sharing the gospel with Jackie. Suddenly she broke down and began sobbing into his chest. He held her close, assuring her that she was loved, and, sensing a raw vulnerability, asked her if she wanted to accept Christ. To his astonishment, she nodded. And she wanted Claire to be the one to pray with her!

As angry as Claire had been, the Holy Spirit replaced her anger with tender forgiveness, and she led her little sister in a prayer of repentance. God had broken through on one of the worst evenings we'd experienced with Jackie. We were haggard and our emotions were depleted, but our joy was full. Whether or not it was a genuine conversion, we can't know. We cling to the hope that Jackie's profession of faith, her years in a loving school and church, and the time spent with our family will prove seed for later fruit. Only God knows.

Jesus Loves the Little (and Broken) Children

Christian parents know there is nothing more important than the salvation of their children. Our adversary has a canny way of wrapping sin in pretty packages, so their gaze is averted from the true beauty of Christ. What can be done, then, to convince our children that God is more attractive than anything the world has to offer?

If your child is enamored with the things of the world, particularly technology and social media, you may find the competition with things of faith seems way too steep. You may be feeling like the sharing of the gospel with your child is falling on deaf ears or that if you sinned in your anger, or didn't handle a crisis well, your witness is blown. Take heart. Your child's salvation is not your responsibility. It's God's.

In the gospel, Jesus tells His disciples to allow children to come to Him (Matt. 19:14).[1] Jesus loves children. Jesus also said that He came not for the righteous, but for those who are sick, both physically and spiritually (Mark 2:17).[2] He loves children and He loves broken people. Jesus loves broken children.

Satan Wants Your Child's Heart

The contest for the hearts of our children is real, literal, and perpetually raging. The enemy does not sleep. He operates with Machiavellian brilliance. We must be intentional, relentless, and confident in our pursuit of Deuteronomy 11:19, 'You shall teach them to your children, talking of them when you are sitting in your house, and when you are walking by the way, and when you lie down, and when you rise.' Failing to indoctrinate our children in the truth of the gospel is antithetical to loving them. What may be a bitter pill or a bore to them now may bring them to a saving faith later.

Salvation Belongs to the Lord

The salvation of your child is completely in the control of the sovereign God who created him. Your job is to steward the best you can in the strength of Christ.

Remember, the gospel promises are for your child too. Nothing, not his mental illness, her poor decisions, his rage,

---

1. 'but Jesus said, "Let the little children come to me and do not hinder them, for to such belongs the kingdom of heaven."'

2. 'And when Jesus heard it, he said to them, "Those who are well have no need of a physician, but those who are sick. I came not to call the righteous, but sinners."'

or your parenting failures, absolutely nothing can separate your child from the love of Christ (Rom. 8:38-39).[3] And nothing you can do can assure your child's salvation. That has been ordained from before time began (Eph. 1:4-5).[4] So you can rest assured that if your child is among the elect, he or she will be saved.

Even though your child's redemption is not in your hands, you mustn't stop hoping for his salvation. There are still steps you must take to walk in the obedience God expects, to bring your child straight to the Throne of Grace.

Pray

Crying out to God is the first and best defense against the mental illness that is binding your child's heart and mind. Prayer is a simple step, but remarkably difficult to carry out at times. Yet it was always the first step Jesus took before a trial or before ministering to people. He knew that apart from His Father, He could do nothing (John 15:5).[5] The desire for your child's salvation must be ultimate, and prayer is the best defense against an enemy who would try to thwart it (as if he could).

1 Thessalonians 5:17 tells us to 'pray without ceasing.' Philippians 4:6 encourages us to 'not be anxious about anything, but in everything by prayer and supplication with thanksgiving let your requests be made known to God.' Perhaps the most poignant scripture for me was Romans 8:26, which tells us, 'the Spirit helps us in our weakness. For we do not know what to pray for as we ought, but the Spirit

---

3. 'For I am sure that neither death nor life, nor angels nor rulers, nor things present nor things to come, nor powers, nor height nor depth, nor anything else in all creation, will be able to separate us from the love of God in Christ Jesus our Lord.'

4. 'For he chose us in him before the creation of the world to be holy and blameless in his sight. In love he predestined us for adoption to sonship through Jesus Christ, in accordance with his pleasure and will' (NIV).

5. 'I am the vine; you are the branches. If you remain in me and I in you, you will bear much fruit; apart from me you can do nothing.'

Himself intercedes for us with groanings too deep for words.' Sometimes, when I prayed for Jackie's heart, groanings were the only utterances I could muster.

In addition to praying for our children's salvation and restoration, praying with our children is essential. Some of my sweetest memories of raising Jackie were of the evening tuck-ins when we would end the day in prayer. When Jackie was lucid and calm, her prayers were eloquent and sincere. Sometimes, the prayers would involve answering her many questions about the things of God. We took advantage of those calm eyes of the storms to show her the goodness of God while she was listening.

Read God's Word

Raising a child with mental illness can leave families in darkness for days and weeks at a time. There were seasons with our daughter when I never thought we would see any light. Her salvation seemed impossible. But the Scriptures told me otherwise, so I relied on them for hope, even when hope seemed dim.

Psalm 119:105 assures us that God's Word is a lamp that lights the path before us.[6] But only at our feet. So we mustn't ever let the lamp go out. We must 'continue in what [we] have learned and have firmly believed' (2 Tim. 3:14). Our way will become dark without the light of the gospel.

Reading God's Word helps us to remember truth, because when we are in the midst of chaos, we are quick to forget. Romans 15:4 says, 'For whatever was written in former days was written for our instruction, that through endurance and through the encouragement of the Scriptures we might have hope.' When we neglect to read the Bible, or when we fail to go to it for comfort and encouragement, when we gaze only

---

6. 'Your word is a lamp for my feet, a light on my path.'

on our circumstances and forget to 'stand by the roads, and look ... for the ancient paths' (Jer. 6:16), doubt creeps in and replaces hope.

Present the Gospel

Our children need to hear God's Word, too. Each summer, difficult as it was, I held Bible study with Jackie. It was never perfect. I didn't always remember to do it, but I limped along in trying to give her as much gospel truth as her heart would hold. I clung to the promise that training her in truth would not return void (Prov. 22:6).[7] Sometimes she listened, but most times she tolerated. But I persevered. I might not ever see the fruit, but I know I did what I could to instill God's absolutes and His message of salvation into her broken soul.

In her talk at the Gospel Coalition women's conference a few summers ago, Kristie Anyabwile spoke of her grandmother, who faithfully took every opportunity to teach her about God — not through formal devotion times, or a curriculum or formula, but by simply and unwaveringly living out her convictions before her granddaughter and speaking the truth to her.

Children will not learn the gospel without hearing it. Not just on Sundays, but every day. Paul asks, in Romans 10:14, 'How then will they call on him in whom they have not believed? And how are they to believe in him of whom they have never heard? And how are they to hear without someone preaching?'

Don't become complacent or succumb to the lie that your schedule is too tight or life too chaotic to regularly share the gospel with your child. Don't let the frustration and anger you may be feeling toward your mentally ill child keep you from it either. When you're driving him to soccer or a counseling

---

7. 'Train up a child in the way he should go; even when he is old he will not depart from it.'

appointment, tucking him into bed, walking through the mall, waiting in line at Chick-fil-A, be intentional in taking every opportunity to teach him sound doctrine through the regular hearing of Scripture and doctrinally sound music. Take every moment with your child captive to the teaching of Christ.

Make Your Joy in Christ Visible

When my children were small, I made it a point to show them the resplendent and dazzling creativity of God. From a magnificent sunset to a lovely vista to a fascinating animal at the zoo, or simply a towering tree or pretty flower in our yard, I would quiz joyfully, 'What is God?' to which they'd shout the blithe reply, 'A good artist!' I wanted to make sure they recognized God's handiwork and glorified Him in His marvelous creativity, genius, and beauty. When God gives you reason to exult, share it with your kids! And don't just do it from the mountaintop. Be sure to remind your children of God's grace and glorify His goodness from the depth of the valleys, as well. Don't waste a moment in showcasing our benevolent God in all circumstances. Your enthusiasm and love for Christ will make an impression on your children.

When we had difficult episodes with Jackie, we were careful to follow up with talks about the goodness of God and how He has helped us come through difficult times. We always wanted her to know that we didn't separate our joy in Christ from the trials we faced. The joy was permanent, the trials fleeting. We also wanted her to see consistency in our faith. If God was good in the good times, we wanted to make sure we showed her His goodness in the struggles.

Go to Church

Going to church wasn't always easy. There were mornings we literally carried Jackie out to the car, kicking and screaming. When she was a teenager, she refused to sit with us in church.

Thank God we had friends there who took Jackie in, making it a point to sit with her and keep her focused on the service. I am forever grateful for those faithful servants who came alongside us in our darkest times.

Later in this book, I will talk about childhood mental illness and the church, but it's important to point out that if you are raising a child who acts out, you will do well to find a church family who will support you without judgment or condemnation, and who have the resources to accommodate your needs. Some churches, good as they may be otherwise, are reticent to accept children with severe emotional challenges. They may simply not have the means or wherewithal to do so.

Our church family was invaluable in our ability to persevere. They gave us comfort, respite, and encouragement throughout every trial and heartache. Church also was another avenue for Jackie to hear the gospel. We couldn't have raised her without it.

Surround Yourself with People Who Will Share in Your Mission

When we were in the darkest times with Jackie, we were weak. There were days I couldn't even speak to her, let alone share the gospel. If we hadn't had friends who were willing to stand in the gap for us, I'm not sure the seed would have been firmly planted. Not only did our friends pray for us, they prayed with us and with Jackie. They took her home with them and showed her Christ's love. Because they were Christ followers, they did not shy away from sharing in the mission to bring Jackie to Him.

You cannot raise a mentally ill child alone. You need God's people surrounding you. If you are like me, you don't like to put people out, or accept help. But going it alone will wear you down. God's strength in your weakness is supernatural, but it is also shown through His people. We learned pretty quickly that we needed help with our daughter, both physically and spiritually. Our friends were a literal godsend.

God loves your child. It is not for us to judge whether or not our children will be saved. It is up to us to do everything we can to show them love, through Christ, and His saving gospel of grace. God will do the rest.

11

Releasing Children to Christre

In middle school, Jackie became obsessed with technology, consumed with going to any lengths to obtain whatever device she could get her hands on. At first, we allowed her to have an iPod. We reasoned that giving her some freedom under our close supervision in a controlled environment would allow her to prove herself capable of handling a device. Though we did not allow her access to social media of any kind, and every device in our home was passworded and locked in our bedroom or a safe when we weren't using them, where there's a will, there's a way, and her will was indefatigable. Her addiction to drama, common in children with traumatic pasts, made her almost manic for social media. When she was online, she was even more unfiltered than in person.

Technology was the number one point of contention in our home throughout Jackie's adolescence. On it, Jackie harassed other children, sent provocative pictures of herself to boys, and ostracized herself from her classmates. With no concept of danger or boundaries, she freely gave our address and phone number to anyone who asked. Parents began calling us complaining that Jackie was stalking or threatening their children. She thrived on the attention and conflict, never taking responsibility, always deflecting the guilt onto others. We ultimately had to ban her from any type of technology, which, despite our herculean efforts, proved daunting and nearly impossible.

Jackie's eighth grade year was a disaster. Her school did their best to keep Jackie from technology, but they couldn't be everywhere. She had managed to get around the school's filters, and started a Facebook page. The internet was a playground for her, a place where she could see whatever she wanted and be seen wherever she wanted. She began acting out sexually online, interacting with anyone who would give her attention. Despite our best efforts to drill into her the dangers of talking to strangers online, her obsession overrode any sort of reason.

At school, behavior reports began stacking up. Inappropriate comments to other students, stealing, and general disruption were taking their toll on the school's resources. In late winter, Jackie was caught with a bottle of hard lemonade which she'd pilfered from our refrigerator. Her intention was to boast to her peers that her parents had alcohol in their fridge, thinking this would cause a major scandal at her tiny Christian school. Her peers turned her in and Jackie was suspended. It was around that time that she began acting out sexually, and her countenance seemed to be perpetually manic. The day she exposed herself to some boys in her class was her last day at the school.

Despite our maximum-security lockdown on technology, Jackie was skilled at either stealing or manipulating devices from peers at her new school and hiding them in her room. We only knew about them if our other children saw that she was online, or when we got calls from people telling us to get Jackie to leave their children alone. One evening, Claire called from college, hysterical with fear. A boy had posted on Jackie's unauthorized Facebook page that he was tired of her stalking and harassing him, so he was going to come to our home and kill her and our family. By the time we got to the bottom of it, Jackie had deleted the post. We called the police and changed our house's security code. Still, we could not convince Jackie of the danger she was putting herself in, such was her craving for drama and attention.

The summer before high school, we began locking down our home. Because Jackie stole from us perpetually, and because of her crazed obsession to obtain a device, we locked every interior door, carrying keys in our pockets. Because the Blu Ray player had access to the internet, we couldn't even allow her to watch TV on her own. We spent hours at the counselor, who encouraged us to get Jackie involved in positive activities. We tried babysitting, but she prompted the eight-year-old boy up the street to strip down and take a bath while she watched. We got her a volunteer job at a local pet shelter, but they had a computer, and instead of doing her job, she got on social media. We couldn't even allow her to volunteer at the church nursery because once she had taken a little girl to the bathroom and stripped her down before placing her on the toilet. We couldn't leave her out of our sight. It felt like prison. For all of us.

Relinquishing Control

Children afflicted with mental illness often require ruthlessly consistent parameters and intense supervision. Whether it's due to anxiety, depression, or impulsive or oppositional behavior, the fallout of their illness may result in harm, either to themselves, others, or to property. From school programming to navigating the mental health system to superintendence at home, parents often must keep close tabs on every detail of their child's life. Relinquishing control can be frightening because circumstances have the potential to unravel quickly. But God can be utterly trusted with our children, because He loves them more than we ever could. Parents can and must surrender their mentally ill child to Christ, even as they endeavor to manage their tenuous circumstances.

I can remember when my son, my firstborn, was an infant, being terrified that something would happen to him. Though I wasn't yet a believer, I would 'pray' over him every night in his crib. My words were more mantra or talisman than prayer, and I compulsively, almost chant-like, recited them hoping they would help to ward off his dying in the night. When I became a believer several years later, the last stronghold I relinquished to the Lord was my children. It took me years to do it. I was fearful that if I gave my children to God, He would pull a Job on me. Of course, that is illustrative of my gross misunderstanding of God's sovereignty, goodness, and compassion. In His kindness, I have come to know that what God ordains is right, and He can be altogether trusted with our lives, and that includes our children. Not to say He wouldn't ordain in His sovereign goodwill something bad happening to them. But I can trust that He would never appoint anything that wasn't good for me and for His kingdom, no matter how painful it might seem. Keeping my children from Him, as if I could, was a foolish exercise in futility.

Startling Trust

Three notable Bible accounts stand out as shining examples of parents entrusting their children to God. Each true story involves surrender in the midst of confusion, fear, pain, and loss. We would do well to aspire to the faith of Abraham, Jochebed, and Hannah.

Abraham's faith astounds me. Genesis 22 gives an account of the epitome of surrendering a child to the Lord. One day Abraham received a command from God: 'Take your son, your only son Isaac, whom you love, and go to the land of Moriah, and offer him there as a burnt offering on one of the mountains of which I shall tell you' (Gen. 22:2). Wait, what? See, this is exactly why I had trouble offering my kids to God when my faith was new. This story is told in fourteen short verses, but imagining the details leaves me incredulous at the scope and magnitude of it. Was Abraham incredulous too? Did he have to ask the Lord to repeat the instructions, doubting that he'd heard Him correctly? It doesn't seem so. Abraham had complete trust in his God, and so he unquestioningly obeyed, trekking toward the destruction of the child God had promised him all those years ago (Gen. 18:10).[1]

Imagine it. Abraham wakes up in the morning, just like any other morning. Isaac is there, most likely rising with his dad to assist in the day's tasks. But instead of tending the animals or chopping wood or stoking the daily fire, Isaac is told to mount up and go with his father. They had to travel three days to get to Mount Moriah by donkey. That's seventy-two hours to think about what he is being sent to do. I wonder if Abraham was calm in his trust, or if he, like I'm sure I would be, needed to fight to settle his reeling mind. Once at their destination, he had to take the time to unsaddle the donkey, explain his intentions to Isaac, lift him onto the altar, then arrange the wood *on top of his son,* looking into his eyes, compelling his boy to trust him as he trusted his heavenly Father. Despite the confusion it must have brought to his temporal mind, Abraham's heart trusted his Father implicitly, and he was able to relinquish control to Him, brandishing a knife and raising it to strike down his only boy. Astonishing! In the end, God stayed Abraham's hand as he raised the knife, and provided the required sacrifice (Gen. 22:13).[2] Abraham passed the test, leaving us with a type of Christ's substitutionary atonement and an astounding example of trust.

We move on to Jochebed, whose story is told in Exodus 2. Pharaoh had commanded all Hebrew baby boys to be drowned in the Nile because he feared the proliferation of the Jews in his land. Jochebed did not heed Pharaoh's command, but rather

---

1. 'The LORD said, "I will surely return to you about this time next year, and Sarah your wife shall have a son."'

2. 'And Abraham lifted up his eyes and looked, and behold, behind him was a ram, caught in a thicket by his horns. And Abraham went and took the ram and offered it up as a burnt offering instead of his son.'

entrusted her son Moses to God. She prepared a basket of bulrushes, slathered it with pitch, placed her boy in the basket and hid him among some reeds in the river, where he was picked up by Pharaoh's daughter. In God's kindness, Jochebed was chosen as a wet nurse for the boy, so she was able to stay in his life, if only for a little while.

Had Jochebed not relinquished her son to the Lord, there would have been no burning bush, no Red Sea, no wilderness journey, and no demonstration of God's power, providence, and compassion for His people. Jochebed's trust in her God resulted in a massive exhibition of the Lord's sovereignty in turning what is meant for evil to good. It might not have been what Jochebed had wanted for her or her son, and there was certainly pain in the surrender, but God's purposes were fulfilled, and good of epic proportions resulted because of her trust.

Finally, we look to Hannah, the mother of Samuel. 1 Samuel 1 and 2 tell the story. Hannah was barren, and pleaded with the Lord for a son. Before the child was even conceived, Hannah entrusted him to God. After caring for him in his infancy, she relinquished him to the Lord, seeing him only once a year when she would bring him a little robe she had made for him. I imagine her thinking about him daily, wondering how he was faring, estimating his size as she lovingly sewed the robe she would give him when she and her husband went up to Jerusalem to offer the yearly sacrifice (1 Sam. 2:19).[3] Again, there is pain involved in the surrender. But what God did in the midst of that pain served His great purposes. In the end, Hannah exulted in prayer:

> The LORD kills and brings to life; he brings down to
> Sheol and raises up. The Lord makes poor and makes

---

3. 'And his mother used to make for him a little robe and take it to him each year when she went up with her husband to offer the yearly sacrifice.'

rich; he brings low and he exalts. He raises up the poor from the dust; he lifts the needy from the ash heap to make them sit with princes and inherit a seat of honor. For the pillars of the earth are the LORD's, and on them he has set the world. (1 Sam. 2:6-8)

God Will Sustain

When we were raising Jackie, it was often hard for me to admit that I didn't have all the answers. After all, I was the teacher, the 'expert.' I worked hard at tending to every detail of her life in order to keep her safe, to heal her trauma, to help her succeed in school, and to somehow teach her to be happy and overcome her past. But the scale of Jackie's illness extended far beyond my ken. I had no choice but to rely on God's strength for her superintendence and for sustenance in the trial.

In an article for *Desiring God*, David Gough wrote:

And all the time, be willing to admit that you do not have all the answers. Despite our strong hold on providence, rarely do we discern with clarity God's mysterious workings in the lives of our children.[4]

In another *Desiring God* article, written primarily for mothers, but applicable to anyone raising afflicted children, Katie Faris explained:

A suffering mother glorifies God when she trusts him, as he uses his Word to sustain her through her trial. My journal from that time begins with a list of verses about trusting God: 'Do not let your hearts be troubled. Trust in God; trust also in me' (John 14:1). 'Blessed is the man who trusts in the LORD, whose confidence is in him' (Jer. 17:7). 'Trust in the LORD forever, for the LORD, the LORD, is the Rock eternal'

---

4. David Gough, 'When a Pastor's Child Strays' (The Gospel Coalition, June 14, 2021). thegospelcoalition.org/article/pastors-child-strays

(Isa. 26:4). Just as God provided daily manna for the Israelites when they wandered in the wilderness for 40 years, a suffering mother who trusts God can expect his mercies to be 'new every morning' (Lam. 3:23).[5]

I found this to be true. With each new day, when I surrendered Jackie's care to the One who created her, I was cloaked in new mercies. Trusting God with our children does not guarantee our myopic expectation of success, nor does it alleviate all the pain and fear in the surrender. But it does guarantee His sustenance and provision in the trial. We can place our confidence in Him because our children are much safer surrendered to the perfect care of the Lord.

---

5. Katie Faris, 'Motherhood Is a Call to Suffer (in Hope)' (The Gospel Coalition, November 13, 2020). thegospelcoalition.org/article/motherhood-call-suffer-hope

12

Navigating the System

In the fall of her ninth grade year, Jackie was placed in an intensive center-based emotional support classroom run by the local public school district. Being around other mentally ill adolescents, however, only fed her drama addiction and sent her into an even deeper spiral. She soon began getting into fights, ostracized herself from almost every peer, and earned a reputation among her teachers, who'd stopped expecting much from her. Even her emotional support teachers did very little school work with her, acting more as camp counselors than educators. She was regressing academically, socially, and behaviorally.

When Jackie was fifteen, her behaviors escalated exponentially. Her hostility toward anyone trying to reach her prevented her from getting the help she so desperately needed. Eventually, she began cutting, just like many of her classmates. We're not certain it would have even occurred to her to slice her flesh 'to alleviate pain' had it not been introduced to her by her peers. On one of her many bedroom searches we discovered razorblades that she had pilfered from the local Dollar store. We had learned she had been sneaking out at night, once jumping off the second floor roof when we began to set the alarm after being threatened. The mental health system could do little to help our family. We couldn't hospitalize her because, though she was cutting regularly, her arms raw and crisscrossed with lacerations, facilities would not admit her because she wasn't actively trying to kill herself. To them, Jackie was just another troubled kid, and apparently not in full-blown crisis mode relative to many of the adolescents passing through their system. Again and again, we were sent home from doctors and the ER after violent self-harming episodes, the only help a prescription to 'up' one or more of her many medications. It got to the point where we were actually hoping she would attempt suicide so we could get her the help that she needed. Eventually, that hope was realized.

Jackie's temper would occasionally lead her to say she was going to kill herself. We always felt she was too narcissistic to actually carry it out, just as we had the sense that her cutting was less a cry for help than a megaphone for attention. However, that didn't mean that in an attempt to get that attention, she wouldn't impulsively and inadvertently do some real harm. It took a gargantuan amount of vigilance to keep her safe.

In the summer before tenth grade, Jackie was in a particularly deep spiral, hateful and depressed. Counseling sessions were reduced to hour-long rants about how horrible we were and how her life was a prison. She expressed her hatred of us on a regular basis, and told anyone who would listen that she just didn't want to live anymore. Still, without an actual suicide attempt or at least a cogent plan of one, the mental health system was impotent to help us. Finally, one afternoon, I found a suicide note she had written in her journal and left open on the stairs. Jackie had drawn a detailed progression of a plan to hang herself from her ceiling fan. Indeed, she had fashioned a noose, which we'd found in her bedroom. That night, she was hospitalized for the first time.

That hospitalization almost didn't happen, however. In Pennsylvania, when a child reaches the age of fourteen, they have almost complete autonomy over their own mental healthcare. A passel of bureaucrats in Harrisburg decided that giving power to a mentally ill fourteen-year-old (let alone any fourteen-year-old) was best practice. They obviously have never lived with a mentally ill adolescent. Any decision that needed to be made regarding medication, counseling, or hospitalization required Jackie's signature of approval. Mind you, though she had all the power, my husband and I had all the responsibility. We were incredulous to think that the mental health system gave that much credence to a child who was suicidal and completely out of touch with reality! Yet we were dependent on that system because we didn't have the financial resources to send her to one of the many elite mental health facilities I had researched.

Insurance, which in reality is the entity that runs the show, only covered a limited number of facilities and interventions, most of which were state subsidized. State subsidized, we found, is almost always synonymous with ineptitude, massive red tape, and poor quality. Only after we explained to Jackie that a voluntary committal to a mental health facility would be expunged from her record when she turned eighteen did she agree to the hospitalization. She knew we had enough evidence to obtain an involuntary committal, which would remain on her record permanently. By God's grace, she exercised enough clarity to make the right decision.

With the procurement of insurance approval, Jackie was transferred by ambulance to an adolescent behavioral health facility forty-five minutes from our home. She stayed in the facility for one month, and was released without any indication that she was better. In fact, the girl they'd returned to us was much worse than the girl we'd taken to the hospital. She had acted out regularly there, even escaping once when a visitor held the door open too long. The staff did not show much integrity, and had made matters worse. We'd learned later that her favorite staff member had been in the habit of regaling her with his homosexual antics on the weekend. They finally released her because they could do nothing more to help her. She didn't want to return to us, so it took five staff members to escort her to our car. My husband sat in the back with her on the ride home because we feared she would try to escape. She remained curled in a fetal position, hiding her face the entire trip. We tried to assure her that we would find her good help, but she resisted any of our attempts to nurture her.

The follow-up plan was to place her in an outpatient day hospital for intensive therapy with other mentally ill adolescents. After one week at the facility, Jackie overdosed on another child's medication, which he had squirreled away in his pocket and was passing out to his fellow patients. Jackie was taken by ambulance to the hospital, strapped to the gurney for her safety. Late that night, she was transported by another ambulance to a behavioral health facility in Allentown, PA, seventy miles from our home in Lancaster. I packed a bag for her and followed the ambulance so I could admit her. She seemed relieved to be away from home, yet getting help. We felt the same way.

The second facility was markedly better, but not nearly what we would have wanted for our daughter. She spent eighteen months there with very little benefit. She returned to us for a short time before deciding to run off to Philadelphia to live with her biological family. It was just before her eighteenth birthday.

When Jackie became pregnant a few months after leaving our home, we had one more go around with the system. I went to be with her for the birth, frantic with worry over her little girl, wondering how Jackie would be able to raise her. The hospital staff understood the situation, and the social worker was called in. Jackie would not be allowed to take her daughter home. Through the incompetence of a Philadelphia social-service worker, who decided my husband and I were not legally entitled to take her home with us, our granddaughter was placed in a foster home somewhere in Philadelphia. It took ten intense days of fighting, phone calls, and multiple trips down to the city before we were finally allowed to bring her home. Late at night, we made the trip back to Philadelphia and met the social worker on the street outside Jackie's shelter, which was wedged between two abandoned buildings in a decaying neighborhood. Waiting in the car on the dark street was disconcerting. Finally, the social worker arrived with the baby, handed her over to us on the street, like some kind of drug transaction, and drove away. The scene was bizarre.

Jackie remained at the shelter, and weekly visits were arranged, as per court order. While Jackie was fighting, unsuccessfully, to get her life in order, we were making arrangements with relatives to adopt the baby should Jackie's parental rights be terminated. Our granddaughter remained in Lancaster for one month, after which, incredibly, during a routine court ordered check-in, the judge decided the baby should be returned to Jackie in the shelter. And that was that.

A Dark System

Out of urgent necessity, many families who are traversing the road of childhood mental illness find themselves becoming unwitting experts on 'the system.' Counselors, case workers, social services, the legal system, and insurance companies thrust parents into a labyrinth of bureaucracy and frustration. The child and adolescent mental health system in America is woefully broken, secular, and dark. Despite hard-working folks toiling in the trenches, the system as a whole does little to help children rise from the mire of their condition. Without unlimited financial resources, families have no choice but to utilize these agencies. Biblical Christian counselors are not always equipped to deal with profound mental illness, or may offer limited insurance options. So Christian parents have little choice but to reach out to secular practitioners. Receiving professional support and assistance may require a dependence on government agencies, or families may find themselves embroiled in scrutiny from social services.

We navigated the system for nine years, and then again when we tried to get help for our granddaughter. We endured scrutiny from a counselor who opined, to Jackie, that we were too strict with our rules, advising us to get Jackie a phone so she 'could be like other kids.' We became subjects of an abuse investigation after we reached out to a psychiatrist. We endured scathing hostility from our daughter during long hours of in-home intensive family therapy. Massive amounts of time, energy, and money were spent desperately trying to find the one right intervention that would help restore our daughter to health.

Refuge in the Lord

If you are in the throes of navigating the child and adolescent mental health system, you may know the frustration and incredulity that assault you with every bad decision the system makes for you. Still, God's counsel for His people does not change, even in the face of being forced to procure secular systems. God's people know that 'it is better to take refuge in the LORD than to trust in man' (Ps. 118:8). And God knows that sometimes the world's systems need to be tapped.

Though many of the interventions we sought for Jackie were unsuccessful, we sensed God's presence powerfully and palpably. We sought Him fervently with every medical and psychiatric decision we had to make. He kept us safe from being taken 'captive by philosophy and empty deceit, according to human tradition, according to the elemental spirits of the world, and not according to Christ' (Col. 2:8). We were given discernment in the tortuous journey, and comfort in the darkest times. God brought to mind scriptures that fueled our determination and trust:

> Seek the LORD and his strength; seek his presence continually. (1 Chron. 16:11)

> Who among you fears the Lord and obeys the voice of his servant? Let him who walked in

darkness and has no light trust in the name of the LORD and rely on his God. (Isa. 50:10)

Ponder the path of your feet; then all your ways will be sure. (Prov. 4:26)

For I, the LORD your God, hold your right hand; it is I who say to you, 'Fear not, I am the one who helps you.' (Isa. 41:13)

As I write this, I am preparing to help Jackie navigate yet another system, that of government assistance. She has tried to strike out on her own, and has found herself in poverty and is soon to be homeless. As I research eligibility for a dizzying plethora of government programs and services, I am reminded that God brought us through the labyrinth once and I know He will be faithful as we enter it again, if we abide in Him (John 15:4)[1] through the process.

A Different Kind of Success

Without the Lord, navigating the child and adolescent mental health system would have been an exercise in pure frustration and sorrow. But through this trial, we discovered that God's promise to give us the desire of our heart if we delight in Him often yields something unexpected. When we delight in God, He leads our hearts to desire Him. Jesus Christ becomes the first and greatest desire of our heart. Then we are able to tap His strength to face the sorrow and frustration with a transcendent peace. Suddenly, no matter the hardship or trial or disappointment, God's grace in the giving of Christ is sufficient for us (2 Cor. 12:9).[2] He lavishes on us His love,

---

1. 'Abide in me, and I in you. As the branch cannot bear fruit by itself, unless it abides in the vine, neither can you, unless you abide in me.'

2. 'But he said to me, "My grace is sufficient for you, for my power is made perfect in weakness." Therefore I will boast all the more gladly of my weaknesses, so that the power of Christ may rest upon me.'

His comfort, His protection, His provision, and His quietude, though the trial remains. When our heart is aligned with His, even and especially in the fiercest of storms, He gives us the desire of our hearts: Him alone.

13

Finding Identity in Christ

Jackie was a child in pain. She couldn't make sense of the lot she was given in life, and her way of coping was to lash out at those around her. Since we were the closest to her, we were the ones who received the brunt of the hostility. In the last year she was with us, we digested a regular diet of vitriol, scathing criticism, and personal affronts. Jackie knew just where to land a verbal punch. She told us daily how stupid we were, and that we weren't fit to raise her. We were too ignorant to understand her issues. We were hypocrites and liars. We'd stolen her away from her family. The personal attacks became so bad that I once stopped a trauma therapy session in which she was raging on and on about our incompetence and loudly expressing her hatred toward us. The counselor had always allowed her to vent, I suppose reasoning it was cathartic for her. But at that moment, the weight of the affronts came crashing down and I had had enough. I insisted the counselor begin to shut down the hostility. It was taking its toll.

God Sings over You

The all-consuming nature of raising a child with mental illness, in which relentless hostility and perpetual opposition can be part and parcel, threaten to erode a parent's sense of worth. Pervasive anger, skewed attachment, or impaired social skills can mean a dearth of affection and affirmation, leaving parents feeling small and inconsequential.

It's hard to fight a battle when you're emotionally depleted and under near constant attack. It took a lot for me not to take what I perceived as our failure with Jackie. I spent many days steeped in denigration over my parenting, motives, and actions. My very identity was under attack. The only thing that brought me out of the mire of self-doubt, and, yes, self-pity was focusing on the promise of God's love for me. Zephaniah 3:17 was particularly helpful:

> The LORD your God is in your midst, a mighty one who will save; he will rejoice over you with gladness; he will quiet you by his love; he will exult over you with loud singing.

When my children were babies, I would sing over them in their crib. This verse brought that to mind as I pictured God singing over me. He loves me that much. Couple these marvelous words with the knowledge that there is not one iota of condemnation or reproach in God's countenance toward us, and it is nearly impossible to feel small and inconsequential! God's promises of love and exultation over me served as a bulwark against the daily hostility that buffeted my heart.

In the Psalms, I learned that God planned for my arrival into this world, and fashioned me just so, and to His exact specifications (Ps. 139:13-15).[1] In the gospels, I was reminded that God cares for every detail of His creation, and His children, of which I am one, are cherished most of all (Luke 12:6-7).[2]

Sliver of Truth

The verbal assaults Jackie pelted at us often contained a sliver of truth, sometimes causing me to fight the urge to question the veracity of them. But the hostility was not the root of

---

1. 'For you formed my inward parts; you knitted me together in my mother's womb. I praise you, for I am fearfully and wonderfully made. Wonderful are your works; my soul knows it very well. My frame was not hidden from you, when I was being made in secret, intricately woven in the depths of the earth.'

2. 'Are not five sparrows sold for two pennies? And not one of them is forgotten before God. Why, even the hairs of your head are all numbered. Fear not; you are of more value than many sparrows.'

my struggling with my identity and worth. It was simply a catalyst.

If we are honest with ourselves, we don't need a lot of help convincing us that we 'fall short of the glory of God' (Rom. 3:23). Because of all the sin and discord in the world that cloys my soul, it is the sin that resides in my own heart and mind that wearies me the most. Insecurities that steal my joy. Lightning-fast rogue thoughts that challenge my faith. Bitterness, mistrust, envy, jealousy, and worry that repeatedly slam into my heart until my soul is battered and bruised. And the salt that rubs deep into the wounds, that keeps them raw and angry, is the abrasive irritant of guilt.

But God, in His expansive love, has provided a formula for combatting the enemy within (and those without). He knows my heart, even the dark parts of it, and He has equipped me with everything I need to stave off condemnation. That heavenly formula is forgiveness, love for enemy, and self-denial.

Forgiveness

When I encounter an enemy, I am commanded to pray for him (Matt. 5:44).[3] So I plead for a forgiving spirit, just like Christ did from the cross (Luke 23:34).[4] The Holy Spirit empowers me to employ that level of forgiveness, and, in fact, Jesus lists it as a requirement for receiving it from the Father (Matt. 6:15).[5]

If the challenge to my worth makes me feel like I am my own worst enemy, it follows that I must extend forgiveness to myself. Not in an effort to absolve myself of guilt, but as a means to obtain the freedom to move forward through the plans God has for me in carrying out His will for my life. Forgiving myself is simply accepting the forgiveness I have

---

3. 'But I say to you, Love your enemies and pray for those who persecute you.'

4. 'And Jesus said, "Father, forgive them, for they know not what they do."'

5. 'but if you do not forgive others their trespasses, neither will your Father forgive your trespasses.'

received through Jesus Christ. If I am focused on my sin and walk in constant condemnation, I cannot be Christ to other people in my sphere of influence, including my daughter. A repentant sinner is a credible and powerful witness to the forgiveness of God.

Love

When I encounter an enemy, I am also commanded to love him (Luke 6:27).[6] So I plead for a loving spirit. The Holy Spirit replaces my hatred and distrust with a supernatural love that emulates that of Christ (John 13:34).[7]

If I am my own Personal Enemy Number One, then I must apply to myself God's principles for loving enemies. What does loving yourself actually mean? I can start with what it doesn't mean. Self-love is not the same as self-esteem. Nowhere in the Bible does God command us to esteem ourselves. Quite the opposite. When God says, 'Love others as you love yourself' (Matt. 22:39), He is not commanding us to show ourselves love. He is making a tacit assumption that we already do.

But while we love ourselves, in the sense that we care for ourselves and strive to make ourselves happy, without Christ in our lives, or even with Him there, we can also have a propensity toward self-loathing. Especially when someone we are trying to love is egging us on to that end. In this regard, we can apply the mandate to 'love our enemies.' Andrew Peterson, in his sweet song *Be Kind to Yourself* wrote:

> How does it end when the war that you're in is just
> you against you against you? Gotta learn to love your
> enemies too. You can't expect to be perfect. It's a fight
> you've gotta forfeit. You belong to me whatever you do,

---

6. 'But I say to you who hear, Love your enemies, do good to those who hate you.'

7. 'A new commandment I give to you, that you love one another: just as I have loved you, you also are to love one another.'

so lay down your weapon, darling. Take a deep breath and believe that I love you. Be kind to yourself. Gotta learn to love your enemies too.[8]

Self-Denial

Self is one of the prevailing weapons the enemy wields against us. Whether we are focusing on self-love or self-loathing, we are perpetually focused on self. The counter weapon, the command from Jesus Christ who was Himself the master wielder of it, is self-denial (Luke 9:23).[9] And just as self-love is not the same as self-esteem, self-denial is not the same as self-deprecation.

Self-denial – that is a profound placing of the needs of others ahead of your own (Phil. 2:3-8) – is self-love.[10] Self-denial is loving yourself because it takes your mind off yourself and places the focus on others, which makes God happy and you happy, which is the crux of loving yourself.

Scott Hubbard, in an article for *Desiring God*, wrote:

> The life we find on the other side of self-denial may look far different from the life we've always known. But it will not—it cannot—be worse. It is a life where we gain a hundredfold more than we ever give up (Mark 10:30). It is a life where we are no longer a broken note in the symphony of the universe, but are rather sounding the part God created us for. It

---

8. Andrew Peterson, 'Be Kind to Yourself' (Spotify. Centricity Music, October 9, 2015). open.spotify.com/track/1

9. 'And he said to all, "If anyone would come after me, let him deny himself and take up his cross daily and follow me."'

10. 'Do nothing from selfish ambition or conceit, but in humility count others more significant than yourselves. Let each of you look not only to his own interests, but also to the interests of others. Have this mind among yourselves, which is yours in Christ Jesus, who, though he was in the form of God, did not count equality with God a thing to be grasped, but emptied himself, by taking the form of a servant, being born in the likeness of men. And being found in human form, he humbled himself by becoming obedient to the point of death, even death on a cross.'

is a life with Jesus: maker of all beauty, redeemer of all brokenness, fountain of all joy. When you deny yourself, you will not lose yourself—not ultimately. You will find yourself. If you want to delight the devil, then refuse to deny yourself. But if you want to defy your ancient foe, if you want to scorn the one who hates your soul, if you want to cut off the arms that would drag you to hell, then bend down and pick up your cross.[11]

Somehow, when I apply God's formula for dealing with enemies, my own Personal Enemy Number One is transformed into Beloved Child of the King, as I lean into His promise of freedom, lost, then found, under the loving grip of the Savior who redeemed me.

Christ Alone Determines Our Identity

When I was about ten years old, my piano teacher told me she thought I would never amount to anything. Six years later, my Literature teacher wrote in my yearbook, 'May the bluebird of happiness … pass you by.' Granted, I wasn't the most diligent student in piano or Literature, but the tenor of the words still stung. To this day, I keep a tiny glass bluebird on my bookshelf as a poignant reminder that the cutting admonition from my teachers did not predict my future, nor do they define my worth.

The voices of others hold powerful sway over our sense of significance. When those voices degrade, renounce, or reject, we can become blind to the truth that only one voice matters. When you are tempted to allow critical chatter, either your own or someone else's, to pin you under the weight of condemnation, look once more to Scripture to be reminded that you are secure in your relationship with Christ. Then consider with sober joy what that means!

---

11. Scott Hubbard, 'Denying Yourself Is Loving Yourself,' *Desiring God* (September 17, 2020). desiringgod.org/articles/denying-yourself-is-loving-yourself

You Are a Child of God

The moment you submitted to the saving grace of Jesus Christ, you became sealed and adopted as a child of the Creator of the universe. Before, you were merely an image-bearing creation of God, infinitely valuable, but a spiritual orphan. Now, you are adopted into His family:

> But to all who did receive him, who believed in his name, he gave the right to become children of God. (John 1:12)

> See what kind of love the Father has given to us, that we should be called children of God; and so we are … Beloved, we are God's children now.' (1 John 3:1-2)

> For my father and my mother have forsaken me, but the LORD will take me in. (Ps. 27:10)

> But you have received the Spirit of adoption as sons. (Rom. 8:15)

Be cheered, because you are taken in by a perfect Father. Need you ever feel worthless?

You Are an Heir

As a sealed and accepted child of God, you are also an heir. 'And if children, then heirs – heirs of God and fellow heirs with Christ.' (Rom. 8:17). In heaven, you have a trust waiting for you. You are heir 'to an inheritance that is imperishable, undefiled, and unfading, kept in heaven for you' (1 Pet. 1:4).

Drink in the words of Jesus: 'Come, you who are blessed by my Father, inherit the kingdom prepared for you from the foundation of the world' (Matt. 25:34). That invitation is for you. Need you ever feel insignificant?

You Are Royalty

'But you are a chosen race, a royal priesthood, a holy nation, a people for his own possession, that you may proclaim the excellencies of him who called you out of darkness into his marvelous light' (1 Pet. 2:9). This is not figurative language. You are literally royalty in a literal kingdom – the only real kingdom. And you are possessed by the all-powerful, all-benevolent, light-filled King.

On earth, Christ was a servant King (John 13:12-14).[12] So on earth, His royal priests serve in His name. In heaven, Christ is the 'King of kings and Lord of lords' (Rev. 19:16). And we will reign with Him:

> If we have died with him, we will also live with him; if we endure, we will also reign with him. (2 Tim. 2:12)

> You have crowned [man] with glory and honor, putting everything in subjection under his feet. (Heb. 2:7-8)

> Do you not know that we are to judge angels? (1 Cor. 6:3)

What might that look like, to judge angels? One day, you will find out. Need you ever feel powerless?

You Are a Refugee and a Sojourner

The moment you acceded to the saving grace of Jesus Christ, you changed citizenship. Earth became a foreign land in which you must dwell until you are called to your real, marvelous, perfect, glorious, light-filled home. Your 'citizenship is in

---

12. 'When he had washed their feet and put on his outer garments and resumed his place, he said to them, "Do you understand what I have done to you? You call me Teacher and Lord, and you are right, for so I am. If I then, your Lord and Teacher, have washed your feet, you also ought to wash one another's feet."'

heaven, and from it [you] await a Savior, the Lord Jesus Christ'
(Phil. 3:20). And while you wait, you serve and proclaim the
gospel of your King. There is a home being specially prepared
for you (John 14:3).[13] Need you ever feel displaced?

The Only Voice That Matters

I suppose my piano teacher was right. I never did amount to
anything. Instead, I became nothing in order to make Christ
everything.

Only Christ, the Word of Life (John 1:1-4),[14] is able to
drown out the negative voices that pervade and persuade. He
assures us, 'Where are your accusers? Has no one condemned
you? Then neither will I' (John 8:10-11, paraphrased). By God's
grace, sealed and secured in the finality of the cross, we are free
to go in the acceptance and assurance of Jesus Christ.

---

13. 'And if I go and prepare a place for you, I will come again and will take you
to myself, that where I am you may be also.'

14. 'In the beginning was the Word, and the Word was with God, and the Word
was God. He was in the beginning with God. All things were made through him,
and without him was not any thing made that was made. In him was life, and the
life was the light of men.'

14

Finding a Support System

A few years back, my husband and I mentored a young couple who were raising two children afflicted with mental illness. Their younger daughter was stricken with childhood onset schizophrenia, and was pretty well regulated with medication. Their older daughter, however, suffered from Reactive Attachment Disorder (RAD), and her illness mirrored Jackie's almost to a tee. This precious family had lost friends, and had ultimately left their church because of a gross lack of understanding over the decisions they had had to make for their daughters. Because many of the interventions and strategies required to help regulate many mentally ill children do not fit into any standard or familiar methods of parenting typical kids, many families are ostracized because of ignorance and rash judgments. Our friends had been almost completely removed from any sort of meaningful interaction with other families because of the misconceptions of others. They were virtually alone.

We took the couple to dinner a few times, and because we could completely relate to their situation, and were all too familiar with the oppressive and gut-wrenching emotions that accompany this road, my husband and I were like an oasis in a friend desert. They expressed over and over how relieved they were to finally find someone who understood. Their loneliness was abated, if only for a little while.

Eliphaz, Bildad, and Zophar

Friends and family can be a great blessing in trial when they are willing to listen more than opine. Job's friends, Eliphaz,

Bildad, and Zophar come to mind. Job was the recipient of great affliction. He lost his home, his livelihood, and worse, his entire family. He was an upright man of faith whom God, in his mysterious good sovereignty, chose to afflict. This is a hard passage of Scripture, one with which I wrestled for years as I came to understand the sovereignty of God. I can't say I'm completely comfortable with God's actions in Job, but that's a commentary for another book.

When Job was first afflicted, his friends traveled to his side, offering quiet support in the form of their presence. 'And they sat with him on the ground seven days and seven nights, and no one spoke a word to him, for they saw that his suffering was very great' (Job 2:13). A couple of chapters later, though, Job's friends decided quiet companionship was not enough to help their friend. One by one, they chose to offer unsolicited (and ignorant) advice. Each friend in turn ventured opinions about the reasons God had inflicted Job with such calamities. Eliphaz reminds Job that God inflicts those who transgress against Him. He offers:

> Remember: who that was innocent ever perished? Or where were the upright cut off? As I have seen, those who plow iniquity and sow trouble reap the same. By the breath of God they perish, and by the blast of his anger they are consumed. (Job 4:7-9)

Bildad suggests that perhaps Job's children got what they deserved:

> If your children have sinned against, him, he has delivered them into the hand of their transgression. If you will seek God and plead with the Almighty for mercy, if you are pure and upright, surely then he will rouse himself for you and restore your rightful habitation. (Job 8:4-6)

Finally, the third friend, Zophar, heaps on the counsel, '[For] he knows worthless men; when he sees iniquity, will he not consider it?' (Job 11:11).

Job's friends were trying to be helpful, instructive even. But in their piousness and zeal for theological accuracy, they swapped compassion (and theological accuracy) for rash judgment, causing their friend more pain.

After publishing two articles on God's sovereignty amidst our challenges with Jackie, I received emails from folks who were struggling with their own mentally ill children. One common theme in some emails was rejection from family, friends, and even church. One woman wrote:

> We found that nobody really understands. Most people will either a) brush it off as nothing since it's too awkward to address properly b) be nosy and ask painful questions that are difficult to answer, often because I don't know the answer or c) (most common and most hurtful of all) they will judge or blame you. But my parents and my biological brother at least knew what I was talking about, so we really made an effort to be united and it wasn't easy, but we are stronger and better because of it.

Another mother told me:

> One of our adopted children suffers from mental illness that manifested itself as extreme violence toward other family members. When he was 14, we had to make the horrifically difficult decision to place him in out-of-home care for the safety of our other children. Our church family at that time was completely unsupportive because, in part, they expected all adoptions by Christian families to end 'happily ever after' here on earth. I so wished that there were more articles like yours available to present all sides of adoption so families experiencing other-than-perfect adoption circumstances would not feel as alone as we did and so that others might begin to comprehend that God is sovereignly at work even

when our prayers for healing are not answered in this life.

And yet another parent wrote:

> I would appreciate a friend! You are so right about only people who have been through this understand. We have even had some close friends judge us so wrongly and unfairly in regards to our parenting ... because we trusted them with our frustrations and venting ... yikes I regret that and have learned.

And another:

> The hardest part for me has been the loneliness of it. Or the hurt of close family making conclusions about our hearts and who we are based on the manipulation of our children. I don't blame them really. I have three master manipulators. My one daughter told my mother-in-law that I scratched her chest in a fit of rage ... she did have a scratch but It [sic] wasn't from me. I could go on and on. The charm and sweetness to strangers, school friends and teachers and then the rage and abuse to me and my husband at home! The Lord is good and has grown me so much! He is creative and teaching me creative ways to get through to my kiddos ... and we are seeing some fruit (however small ... I am thankful).

If you have never lived with a mentally ill child, you have no frame of reference for parenting them. Even parents of strong-willed children cannot begin to comprehend the intensity of raising a child who has profound disconnects in logic, is devoid of empathy, or is lacking any semblance of a conscience. Or one who is debilitated by inexplicable fear.

Finding Help

Finding people who will come alongside you as you navigate the lonely road of childhood mental illness may be daunting.

In the midst of the tempest, you feel battered and alone, and reaching out to people may seem like just one more difficult task you have to maneuver or burden you have to bear. But finding the right people to walk with you is crucial to your own sense of well-being – and your child's. Jackie enjoyed the respite from us every bit as much as we did.

Even if you have no family or friends to help, a Bible-revering church is a good option. If the church is being the church, then they will help any way they can. I would suggest pounding the pavement (or the internet) to find a pastor who will lead his church in 'being the church' to you and your child.

John Knight, a father of an autistic son, writes extensively on the topic of the church and disability. In an article for *Desiring God*, he wrote:

> The saddest stories I hear from parents raising a child with a disability don't involve schools, insurance companies, or hospitals. The stories that elicit the most bitter words, and tears, are the ones about churches that abandon families with a disabled child because they are 'just too difficult to deal with.' This really happens. Too many parents are told, directly and indirectly, by a pastor or church leader or Sunday school volunteer: *You do not belong here.* This is something no people should hear from their church. This is something that should never cross the lips of ministry leaders – not if they really believe what the Bible says about God's sovereignty and good design in disability. But with that said, sometimes churches can be perplexed or even frightened by the issue of disability. Some churches might not know what to do, even though they love God and his word. In instances like this, when the church is centered on the gospel, we can show our confidence in God by being patient

– by trusting God to grow the church and work in the hearts of its leaders.[1]

As exhausted as you might be, persistence (and patience) with a Bible-revering church may win the day. You need help. The church is called to give it to you. John Piper preached, 'You don't have Christians in need when other Christians have plenty. That's what church is! That's what it's for. We will be there for each other. Then you'll find out who church is.'[2]

If your child is adopted, there may be resources through your adoption agency that offer respite for you and for your child. Typical agency respite involves families who are willing to take children for a day or weekend, providing activities for the children and a sweet break for their parents. This may not be ideal, but taking advantage of such resources may be imperative in providing you with care for your own mental health and well-being. Although this is a good option, we found that there was a lengthy waiting list for agency-based respite. There is a supply and demand challenge in the system, at least in our case.

Accepting Help

Accepting help can be hard. One of the greatest challenges we faced in finding a support system was not the lack of people willing to help, but our willingness to burden other people with our daughter's care. God provided us with the friendship of three couples who were willing, despite the intense inconvenience, to take Jackie for weekend visits so my husband and I could regroup. Even when Jackie overflowed one couple's bathtub and flooded their downstairs, even when

1. John Knight, 'Four Kinds of Churches Worth Leaving,' *Desiring God* (March 10, 2014). desiringgod.org/articles/four-kinds-of-churches-worth-leaving

2. John Piper, 'The Church Is Not a Social Club,' *Desiring God* (September 11, 2017). desiringgod.org/messages/what-is-the-recession-for/excerpts/the-church-is-not-a-social-club

she cut the hems off the other couple's daughter's dress-up clothes (to make them shorter), they continued to support us. We made the decision not to have Jackie stay with those sweet friends after those incidents, but their willingness never faltered.

Our family was supportive, as well. My husband's brother and his wife live in our neighborhood, and they showed nothing but love and kindness toward Jackie, allowing her to walk to their house and spend time cooking or doing her nails with my sister-in-law. Our own children, adults by the time Jackie was a teenager, helped by taking her on overnights or at least for a day. It was never easy. She stole from them, destroyed their belongings, and was generally a handful on every visit. But it blessed us beyond measure to see our children loving and honoring us in that way.

Our church can be lifted as a model for churches who support families with afflicted children. Sunday after Sunday, our church family at Grace Baptist Church in Millersville, Pennsylvania, loved us. They assured us of their continued prayers for our family and for Jackie. They never failed to ask how we were doing. We received phone calls and emails from congregants and elders on a regular basis. There was a season in Jackie's adolescence when she'd refused to sit in church with us. Several members took it upon themselves to invite Jackie into their pew. We would often find them sitting with an arm around her shoulder, or talking and smiling with her before the service began. After a godly elderly member of our church went home to Jesus, we were told that Jackie's name was written throughout her journal. When I felt like a failure, or wondered what people must be thinking of our parenting, our church family dispelled my self-deprecation and made me feel loved and validated.

The associate pastor at Grace grew up in a family who took in foster children, two of whom had serious mental illness. He watched those children grow to take advantage of his parents. They consumed their lives, took their money, and offered no remorse or repentance. When Jackie left, and we decided not to pursue her, he offered sympathy from an experienced heart. If there were people at Grace who disagreed with our decision, they never expressed it. We received nothing but support, prayers, compassion, and empathy. We never felt forgotten, even weeks and months after Jackie left. The hugs and handshakes of support and assurances of prayer continued throughout the subsequent years, and still continue to this day. For us, the love and care we witnessed toward us and our daughter offered a warmth and relief that felt like it was from Christ Himself. Our church was being the body of Christ!

The Bible tells us to bear one another's burdens (Gal. 6:2).[3] Christ taught us that the greatest act of love we can extend to another is to lay down our own lives (John 15:13).[4] And Ecclesiastes instructs:

> For if they fall, one will lift up his fellow. But woe to him who is alone when he falls and has not another to lift him up! Again, if two lie together, they keep warm, but how can one keep warm alone? And though a man might prevail against one who is alone, two will withstand him – a threefold cord is not quickly broken. (Eccles. 4:10-12)

If you have someone you trust, who will not judge or criticize your parenting, who will lend a listening ear and provide respite when you are at the end of yourself, take advantage of their care. Accepting help from friends or fellow church members is actually a ministry in itself, and takes great humility. You are giving a brother or sister an opportunity to be Christ to you.

---

3. 'Bear one another's burdens, and so fulfill the law of Christ.'

4. 'Greater love has no one than this, that someone lay down his life for his friends.'

15

Helping Children Fight Fear

I clung to my mother, nearly breaking skin as I sunk my fingers into her arm. Trembling, heart pounding, terrified, I buried my face into her lap. She sat helplessly, stroking my hair and talking softly to me until I grew calm. The source of my terror? Absolutely nothing.

My anxiety attacks began when I was about nine. Years later, when my daughter Claire was about the same age, I was devastated to discover that she began experiencing the same symptoms. The manifestation was almost identical and, as I came to learn, hereditary. I could understand why I had developed chronic anxiety. My mother was stricken with mental illness, so insecurity, inconsistency, and discord were the norm in my home. But Claire was raised in a stable home, with two parents who, though flawed, offered her security and stability. It turns out when a child experiences trauma, the effects extend to the molecular level, and can be passed down through the generations. For the first time in my life, however, I was grateful for that personal monster of mine, because I could relate completely to what my daughter was experiencing. Nevertheless, it was heartbreaking to watch relentless anxiety rob Claire of joy.

That period of Claire's childhood, when the anxiety seemed to devour her vivacity, was painful. The first indication that something was wrong was on a trip to Chicago, when suddenly Claire was terror-stricken because she found herself unable to swallow. With every attempt to eat, her sweet green eyes would widen in pleading panic as she tried to will her throat to work the food down, fearful of choking. Often, she would have to spit the food out and abandon the effort. It was hard not to become frustrated, because a meal could take up to an hour to complete, with very little progress in finishing her food.

When we returned from our trip, I took her to the doctor. There didn't seem to be anything physically wrong with her, so the doctor concluded that it was some sort of acute anxiety. Eventually, we had to limit her food offerings to apple sauce or smoothies or even ice cream. My sister-in-law and I once coined the phrase, 'mortal mother thoughts,' referring to those worst-case scenario worries that often invade a mother's heart. Powerful mortal mother thoughts fast forwarded my mind's eye to Claire's living a life of debilitating anxiety attacks and subsequent eating disorder. Only prayer calmed my fear over these grim projections, helping me to stay in the moment and work to find a solution.

Through the years of her childhood, Claire wrestled with sporadic bouts of anxiety. The swallowing issue lasted several months and eventually resolved, but the anxiety remained. To her credit, Claire did not allow the anxiety to keep her from life. I can remember a time when she was twelve acting in a play at a local community theater, and while on stage was stricken with anxiety. I was in the audience, and knew at once from her expression that she was in the throes of an attack. She never once stopped singing or dancing, and to anyone but her mother, things appeared perfectly normal. After the curtain call, I rushed to her dressing room and told her how proud I was of her for persevering through the trial. That perseverance was key to getting through her affliction throughout most of her life.

When I became a believer in my thirties, getting to know Christ led me to freedom from anxiety. (I could fill another entire book on that battle alone.) But my transformation did not stop my daughter's scourge of irrational and unfounded fear, and my husband and I were faced with the daunting task of helping her come out on the other side.

Fear

All children experience fear. Fear is a good gift from God, meant to warn of danger and to identify and stay within the good parameters God has put into place for the spiritual safety and happiness of His children. Fear was given as a gift to us, but was never intended to be part of our spirit. 'For God gave us a spirit not of fear but of power and love and self-control' (2 Tim. 1:7).

But in the case of clinical anxiety, when fear becomes out of proportion to the challenge or stress that is causing it, children can become slaves to it. The National Institutes of Health reports that up to 25 percent of American children are diagnosed with some type of clinical anxiety.[1] It manifests in a vast number of forms, from the most common, generalized anxiety disorder (GAD), to phobias like separation, crowds, meeting new people, or even a rare phobia like Claire's and mine, vomiting. No matter the source of the fear, however, the common thread is that the fear is irrational and intense, and, if left unchecked, debilitating.

According to the World Health Organization, there has been a 25 percent increase in anxiety since the onslaught of Covid. This has prompted many countries to include mental health initiatives in their Covid response plans. The report states, 'Loneliness, fear of infection, suffering and death for oneself and for loved ones, grief after bereavement and financial worries have also all been cited as stressors leading to anxiety and depression.'[2]

---

1. 'Anxiety in Children,' Effective Health Care (EHC) Program. Agency for Healthcare Research and Quality (September 13, 2016). effectivehealthcare.ahrq.gov/products/anxiety-children/research-protocol

2. 'Covid-19 Pandemic Triggers 25% Increase in Prevalence of Anxiety and Depression Worldwide' (World Health Organization: March 2, 2022). who.int/news/item/02-03-2022-covid-19-pandemic-triggers-25-increase-in-prevalence-of-anxiety-and-depression-worldwide

Covid is just one among many factors we can point to in this cultural moment. Social media, attack on the family, celebration of narcissism, glorifying and even encouraging mental health disorders (think the provision of 'safe spaces' for the anxious or the militant expectation of the social acceptance of gender dysphoria), along with the rejection of Judeo-Christian principles are among them. Anxiety is one bit of the fallout resulting from events outlined in the Bible for the time winding down to the Lord's glorious appearing. Any one of the events prophetically described in Scripture could be a catalyst to the alarming uptick in angst among God's unredeemed (and redeemed) image bearers. Take 2 Timothy 3:1-5:

> But understand this, that in the last days there will come times of difficulty. For people will be lovers of self, lovers of money, proud, arrogant, abusive, disobedient to their parents, ungrateful, unholy, heartless, unappeasable, slanderous, without self-control, brutal, not loving good, treacherous, reckless, swollen with conceit, lovers of pleasure rather than lovers of God, having the appearance of godliness, but denying its power.

Any time God's creation is out of step with the good things He has ordained for it, there will be angst. Nothing will work as it should, including the chemicals in our brain that regulate the good gift of fear.

When our daughter began having anxiety attacks, we were at a loss for how to help her. Through trial, error, and plenty of prayer, we found five things that worked to release her from the bondage of fear, enabling her to grow into a competent, joy-filled, and virtually anxiety-free adult.

Listen

Nothing says love like a good listening ear. Proverbs 18:15 says, 'The ear of the wise seeks knowledge.' Really listen to your child. Nod your head, repeat back to them what they said, make eye contact, and sit quietly. This is not the time to offer advice. Just let them talk, and make sure they know that you have heard them.

Acknowledge

Honesty, indeed, is the best policy. There is no need to deny or sugarcoat the intensity of the irrational fear of an anxiety attack. But while you are acknowledging the fear, don't give it credence. Help them to see that God is bigger. Teach your child to push through it, facing the fear head on. Don't resist it. Rather, ride it out. It will pass.

You might have them recite Philippians 4:13 with you: 'I can do all things through him who strengthens me.' Like all emotions, fear and anxiety are more than just psychological experiences. They often manifest physically, as well. Simply encouraging your child to breathe deeply and slowly in through their nose and exhale through the mouth may help tremendously. Remind your child that they can do this any time they feel afraid, and to meditate on the truth of what they are meditating on.

Keep Perspective and Keep Moving

Whenever Claire would become stricken with anxiety, I would say to her, 'Tell yourself the truth.' In other words, it is important during anxiety attacks to keep perspective. Look around – look outside yourself – and see what is really happening. Is there really anything in that moment to be afraid of? Together, list everything in that moment that you know as truth.

Remind your child that their enemy is 'the father of lies' (John 8:44),[3] and that their heavenly Father is the only One whose voice is worth listening to. Teach your child that their

---

3. 'You are of your father the devil, and your will is to do your father's desires. He was a murderer from the beginning, and does not stand in the truth, because there is no truth in him. When he lies, he speaks out of his own character, for he is a liar and the father of lies.'

strength comes from Christ, while fear is from the enemy (2 Tim. 1:7).[4] Tell them about Peter and the waves, encouraging them to focus on Christ, so they can walk on the water of joy and freedom from fear (Matt. 14:28-33).

Pray

When your child starts to feel anxious, stop everything and pray with them. This is a golden opportunity to help them realize the importance of prayer. It's a good reminder for us as parents, too. Teach your child to go to God with their fears. Instill in them Scriptures that they can hearken back to when they are anxious:

> Do not be anxious about anything, but in everything by prayer and supplication with thanksgiving let your requests be made known to God. (Phil. 4:6)

> Casting all your anxieties on him, because he cares for you. (1 Pet. 5:7)

> The Lord your God is in your midst, a mighty one who will save; he will rejoice over you with gladness; he will quiet you by his love; he will exult over you with loud singing. (Zeph. 3:17)

Work together to commit these Scriptures to memory. Claire told me that memorizing key verses, particularly Philippians 4:6, was pivotal in helping her calm down and keep moving whenever anxiety threatened to paralyze her.

Focus on Christ

Modern culture places children at the center of the universe – both their own and everyone else's. But this is not biblical. Our children must be taught that Christ is the center, that everything we do must glorify Him, and that in doing so, we

---

4. 'For God gave us a spirit not of fear but of power and love and self-control.'

will be given great joy and peace. When we model for our children confidence in Christ (as opposed to modeling a spirit of fear and self-focus), we are training them up in the way they should go (Prov. 22:6).[5]

Being allowed to exit life (staying home from school, isolating from friends, ceasing all activity) in response to anxiety is, I feel, an error too many parents make. It has been my daughter's and my experience that when we stay in the game, focusing on Christ and telling ourselves the truth, we come out the other side stronger, more resilient, and closer to our only source of peace.

Our greatest fear must be of the Lord Himself because God is holy, terrible, and great. Our lives are in His hands whether we realize it or not. 'And do not fear those who kill the body but cannot kill the soul. Rather fear him who can destroy both soul and body in hell' (Matt. 10:28). We can't stop there, though. Because any redeemed sinner knows that while God is indeed holy, terrible, and great, He is also infinitely good. Those of us who follow Christ need to only fear God in the sense that we revere Him and are in profound awe of His holiness and sovereignty. Christ's blood has washed us into the safety of God's goodness, so we have no need to fear His wrath. 'The fear of the Lord is a fountain of life, that one may turn away from the snares of death' (Prov. 14:27). 'The fear of the Lord leads to life, and whoever has it rests satisfied; he will not be visited by harm' (Prov. 19:23).

Every attempt must be made to show your children that God is more real than their fears. He loves them and will delight in quieting and quelling their anxiety with the unsurpassable love of Christ. Freedom from fear through focus on Christ is a gateway to joy, the only joy permanent and powerful enough to overcome stubborn strongholds like fear.

---

5. 'Train up a child in the way he should go; even when he is old he will not depart from it.'

16

Message for the Church

In an article for the ERLC, Dr. Stephen Grcevich, author of *Mental Health and the Church* wrote:

> In my experience, families in which a child or parent is being treated for a mental health condition are significantly less likely to regularly attend worship services or participate in small groups, Christian education, or service activities than their friends or neighbors. Given that one in five children and adults in the U.S. experience at least one mental health condition at any given time, their families represent a large population desperately in need of tangible expressions of the love of Christ and the spiritual benefits associated with active participation in the life of a local church. Families touched by mental illness represent an enormous potential mission field literally living within the shadows of our steeples. A first step for pastors and church leaders seeking to minister to them is to identify potential obstacles to their participation in worship services and other activities most critical for discipleship within your church and consider how those obstacles might be overcome.[1]

Families with mentally ill children often exclude themselves from church because churches, by and large, are not equipped

---

1. Stephen Grcevich, 'Seven Reasons Why Church Is Difficult for Those Touched by Mental Illness' (ERLC. Ethics and Religious Liberty Commission, January 22, 2018). erlc.com/resource-library/articles/seven-reasons-why-church-is-difficult-for-those-touched-by-mental-illness

to accommodate emotional or behavioral needs. Indeed, though our church doesn't have a specific disabilities ministry, it was because many of the members forsook personal comfort in favor of loving Jackie that we were able to attend regularly with her. Churches will do well to create systems that would make gathering more accessible to families who desperately need the fellowship and instruction of the church and its body.

Choosing to Be Christ's Body

Jesus' ministry, which we are called as a body to emulate, was messy and dangerous. He touched lepers, confronted the demon-possessed, and was powerfully drawn to those whom most considered to be the dregs of society. No whitewashed antiseptic ministry for Him. I'm sure it hurt sometimes. I'm sure He was tired and maybe even a little reticent or frightened, even as He drew confidence from His inextricable connection to His Father.

In his book *Gentle and Lowly,* Dane Ortlund wrote:

> [The] high and holy Christ does not cringe at reaching out and touching dirty sinners and numbed sufferers. Such embrace is precisely what he loves to do. He cannot bear to hold back. We naturally think of Jesus touching us the way a little boy reaches out to touch a slug for the first time – face screwed up, cautiously extending an arm, giving a yelp of disgust upon contact, and instantly withdrawing. This is why we need the Bible. Our natural intuition can only give us a God like us.[2]

If you think about it, the only people who repulsed Jesus were the kind of people who *wouldn't* try to love and serve the unlovable. Those who refused to touch the unclean in

---

2. Dane C. Ortlund, *Gentle and Lowly: The Heart of Christ for Sinners and Sufferers* (Wheaton, IL: Crossway Books, 2021), p. 24.

the name of the God they were called to serve. But we are to conform ourselves to His likeness. And that means pain, messiness, and suffering:

> For it has been granted to you that for the sake of Christ you should not only believe in him but also suffer for his sake. (Phil. 1:29)

> If anyone would come after me, let him deny himself and take up his cross and follow me. (Matt. 16:24)

> Whoever says he abides in him ought to walk in the same way in which he walked. (1 John 2:6)

> For to this you have been called, because Christ also suffered for you, leaving you an example, so that you might follow in his steps. (1 Pet. 2:21)

> Be imitators of me, as I am of Christ. (1 Cor. 11:1)

> Therefore be imitators of God, as beloved children. And walk in love, as Christ loved us and gave himself up for us, a fragrant offering and sacrifice to God. (Eph. 5:1-2)

> ... to put off your old self, which belongs to your former manner of life and is corrupt through deceitful desires, and to be renewed in the spirit of your minds, and to put on the new self, created after the likeness of God in true righteousness and holiness. (Eph. 4:22-24)

> You call me Teacher and Lord, and you are right, for so I am. If I then, your Lord and Teacher, have washed your feet, you also ought to wash one another's feet. For I have given you an example, that you also should do just as I have done to you. Truly, truly, I say to you, a servant is not greater

than his master, nor is a messenger greater than the one who sent him. If you know these things, blessed are you if you do them. (John 13:13-17)

For those whom he foreknew he also predestined to be conformed to the image of his Son, in order that he might be the firstborn among many brothers. (Rom. 8:29)

For as many of you as were baptized into Christ have put on Christ. (Gal. 3:27)

Have this mind among yourselves, which is yours in Christ Jesus. (Phil. 2:5)

'For who has understood the mind of the Lord so as to instruct him?' But we have the mind of Christ. (1 Cor. 2:16)

John Piper said, 'It's natural to move away (from people with disabilities). We're not natural. We're Christians!'[3] The church community can choose to either be like the Pharisees, clinging to the comfortable tidiness of their whitewashed religious practices, or they can choose to be the body of Christ, lowering themselves into the dirty, messy reality of the human condition.

Helping a family who is hurting and weary from the perpetual confusion and chaos that accompany raising a child with mental illness can be a blessing to you when you follow Christ's commands to deny yourself for the sake of another. From dropping an encouraging note in the mail, to cooking meals, to offering prayers, to providing respite or just a listening ear, to, better still, creating full-on programs that will accommodate the peculiar needs of the mentally ill, taking on

3. John Piper, 'Don't Look Away from Disability,' *Desiring God* (May 26, 2017). desiringgod.org/messages/why-was-this-child-born-blind/excerpts/dont-look-away-from-disability

the burden of a family in the midst of the struggle with mental illness is being the church, and the very hands of Christ.

Where to Start

Meeting the infinitely varied needs of congregants through church programming is a momentous task. Still, excluding individuals because of disability is antithetical to Scripture. Jesus said:

> When you give a dinner or a banquet, do not invite your friends or your brothers or your relatives or rich neighbors, lest they also invite you in return and you be repaid. But when you give a feast, invite the poor, the crippled, the lame, the blind, and you will be blessed, because they cannot repay you. For you will be repaid at the resurrection of the just. (Luke 14:12-14)

Pastor Jason Meyer of Urban Refuge Church preached, 'A disability is a trumpet blast testifying to your belief in God's sovereignty that even the most severe disability is part of God's good design.'[4] In his book, *Disability and the Gospel*, Michael Beates wrote:

> [T]he church needs to be the place where all people, no matter their situation, can come to find help, mercy, grace, and hope.[5]

Calvary Church in Lancaster, PA, is one such church. Calvary has an excellent and thriving disabilities ministry. They provide one-to-one buddies to children with disabilities so they can be included in Sunday school and other church programs. Mentors are provided to teens and young adults

---

4. Jason Meyer, Bethlehem Baptist Church (March 15, 2014). bethlehem. church/sermon/the-next-generation

5. Michael S. Beates, 'Chapter Nine: What the Church Must Say to the World in the Twenty-First Century,' *Disability and the Gospel: How God Uses Our Brokenness to Display His Grace* (Wheaton, IL: Crossway, 2012), p. 128.

who want to participate in the various ministries at this 1,500+ member church. There is also a 'self-contained' class for developmentally disabled adults, which provides ability appropriate biblical instruction, and social events. In addition, there is a small group for mothers of kids with disabilities, which ministers to the mothers through Bible studies while also providing care and programs for the children. And finally, the church provides a sensory room manned by volunteers who help children with sensory challenges who might need 'a short break from their classroom to regulate their bodies and take a brain break.' The space is also used to 'help our kids engage in Bible learning at a pace and understanding level that meets their unique needs.' Any one of these programs requires people to run them, and the church perpetually posts pleas for volunteers.[6] My brother, Tim, volunteered in the adult ministry at Calvary. When I asked him how he felt about volunteering, he said working with the people 'is humbling and rewarding. [It] puts everything in perspective. They need guidance. I never felt God's presence more than in that class.'

McLean Bible Church in McLean, Virginia, is another church that has a large and established disability ministry.[7] Its founder, Lon Solomon, has a daughter with significant disabilities, so providing opportunities for all people to engage in church, no matter their age or ability, was near to his heart. I toured this massive, 10,000-member church a few years ago, and was overwhelmed by the scale of their disability ministry. The Sunday school classrooms resemble special education classrooms in schools. They provide well-

---

6. 'Disability Ministry: Calvary Church: Lancaster, PA' (Calvary Church | Lancaster, PA). Accessed August 2, 2022. calvarychurch.org/ministries/disability-ministry

7. 'Special Needs' (McLean Bible Church, May 10, 2022). mcleanbible.org/tysons/special-needs

equipped sensory spaces and vetted volunteers to staff each program. There are programs from ages two to adult, and parents have the choice to enroll their child in self-contained classes or allow them to be included in 'regular' Sunday school. The third Friday of every month, the church provides 'Friday Night Respite' for kids 'aged 2-15 with special needs and their typically developing siblings, giving their parents a much-needed break.' There is a 'Friendship Club' for teens, and a day program for adults with disabilities, which has as its goals 'spiritual formation, literacy, vocational training, personal care and independence, recreation and leisure, social skills, travel training and community navigation, and self-advocacy.'

Finally, and most remarkably, McLean is affiliated with Jill's House, started by Lon Solomon and named for his daughter.[8] The goals of Jill's House are not only to provide services for the individuals with disabilities but also to offer respite for families exhausted from the intensity of their children's care. Even overnight!

When Lon Solomon's wife, Brenda, had the dream to begin Jill's House, she remembered declaring, 'I just knew God was going to do it. I didn't know how it was going to happen, but I knew he was going to do it.'[9] And our ever faithful God mightily fulfilled the dream He had given her. After seemingly insurmountable hurdles, which included resistance from the neighbors where the house was to be built, financial constraints, and zoning challenges, Brenda Solomon's dream was finally realized. In 2007, ground was broken for this beautiful facility, which opened in 2010. Lon Solomon said he constantly reminded himself that God is bigger than the neighbors, the county, and their poverty. Faith-fueled persistence led to one of the most impressive disability

---

8. 'Jill's House 10th Anniversary' (McLean Bible Church, October 20, 2020). mcleanbible.org/stories/jills-house-10th-anniversary

9. Ibid.

ministries in the country. Not only do parents receive much needed rest and respite, but the children get to experience activities they would typically be excluded from otherwise. The director of Jill's House explained, 'Many of our kids don't get invited to birthday parties or sleepovers, but here at Jill's House, kids get to have those experiences.'[10]

Parents who have been blessed to participate in McLean's ministries feel relief and a deep sense of care:

> At the point I was starting to look into Jill's House, [my son] had never been invited to a sleepover. That broke my heart because sleepovers are such a natural part of growing up. For that reason, the possibility of Jill's House was very enticing!
>
> I love being a part of a community that I can grow in and trust to give me the rest I don't get anywhere else. Up until that time, I had not had the chance to experience a break of that nature. It was so important for me to access that type of rest – to know myself in a different way. You forget who you are when you never get a break.
>
> When [our son] was diagnosed, it was a crisis of faith: what does this mean for our family? Knowing that Jill's House is a community that is for us, to give us rest, is refreshing and important. It is reliable and consistent. I can count on coming frequently and receiving rest so much more than I otherwise would.[11]

The ministries of Calvary and McLean are geared toward individuals with physical and intellectual disabilities. But the principles that drove the desire to begin the ministries apply to children with mental illness too. Each disability has its own unique challenges. But each church serves the same powerful God.

---

10. Ibid.

11. 'Stories | Jill's House' (Jill's House). Accessed August 3, 2022. jillshouse. org/Stories

Your church might not have the massive financial and human resources of a Calvary or McLean. But no matter how small or financially strapped, your church has the same Savior. Your calling to love the unlovable is identical. And your help comes from the very same power that raised Jesus from death. We find our greatest strength in our most profound weakness, so you are in prime position to step out in faith!

SECTION THREE

Hope for the Journey

17

Beautiful Narrative

Our life with Jackie was more than a journey. It was an odyssey of joys and pain that began with great hope, endured through great trial, ended in great heartache, and resulted in a greater love for Christ, who sustained us through it all.

The Painting and the Narrative

God uses the brush strokes of trial to paint beauty in the lives of His children. Raising a child with mental illness is akin to viewing a painting close up. Stand too close, and the art has no meaning. Stand back, and the picture suddenly makes sense, revealing light, and color, and loveliness.

Soon after Jackie left our home, my husband and I felt lost, reeling with emotional and even physical pain. We wondered what God's intentions were for this trial that He had so clearly ordained. We had poured nearly a decade into our daughter, hoping against hope that she would be healed. The healing never came. We were left emotionally, physically, and spiritually spent.

In the years since raising Jackie, God has gently pulled us back to finally see the full painting that He had commissioned. The beauty is stunning. Between the angry black strokes and dark smudges of our trials, there are bright swathes of color, great splashes of yellows, sky blues, and brilliant emerald greens flecked with gold. The media God used were varied. The sweet evenings of tuck-ins, storytime, and prayer with Jackie.

The selflessness of friends scooping Jackie up for a day or weekend. The perseverance of Dayspring Christian Academy, partnering with us for years to help Jackie learn and grow, and to lay the biblical foundation we hope she will return to and that will sustain her throughout her life. The faithfulness of family who endured the trial alongside us. The love and care of Grace Baptist Church. And especially, the Artist Himself, ever faithful, always guiding, never leaving, and constantly near.

Heartache and trial in the hands of God can yield a beautiful narrative that weaves the pain and distress into a story that tells of His love, faithfulness, and sufficiency. In our searching for answers, beyond relying on God's goodness and sovereignty, we eventually found our beautiful narrative, written before Jackie ever came into our life, and continued throughout our time with her and continuing even now.

God created us (Gen. 1:27). He is with us, His love quiets us, and He sings over us (Zeph. 3:17). He hasn't guaranteed us an easy life, but promises that He has overcome the world (John 16:33). He loves us to death (John 3:16). He wants us to rejoice in Him, He will provide us abundant peace, and He will supply our every need (Phil. 4:19). He wants what is best for us, and works for our good (Jer. 29:11; Rom. 8:28). He will comfort us in our need (Ps. 23:1-6; 2 Cor. 1:3-4). He is completely trustworthy (2 Sam. 7:29; Ps. 9:10). He hears us when we speak to Him (Ps. 31:22). He has accepted us as His own children (Gal. 4:6-7; John 1:12). And He will give us the desires of our heart (Ps. 37:4).

Our Greatest Desire

For some reading this, that last statement might provoke protest. Our daughter left in a flurry of hostility. We are grieving that loss, reeling from the failure. It seems we did not get what our hearts desired. But through this trial, we have discovered that God's promise to give us the desire of our heart if we delight in Him often yields something unexpected. When we delight in God, He leads our hearts to desire Him. Jesus Christ becomes the first and greatest desire of our heart.

Suddenly, no matter the hardship or trial or disappointment, God's grace in the giving of Christ is sufficient for us (2 Cor. 12:9).[1] He lavishes on us His love, His comfort, His protection, His provision, and His peace. They are all unfathomable gifts, but our heart's desire is to have Him and Him alone.

Christ is, and continues to be, faithful, and His affirmation has been clear. At this writing, Jackie is living seventy miles away from us. She is struggling. We continue to try to help her as best we can. We are thankful that she is no longer hostile toward us, and has even apologized to everyone in the family. One of the sweetest days of my life was when Jackie and Claire reconciled and forgave each other. Claire told me recently that for the first time in her life with Jackie, she can honestly say she enjoys her as her sister. What a sweet demonstration of the kindness of our Savior.

We pray every day that Jackie will be able to thrive, and ultimately come to rely on the God she was introduced to when she was little. We see her trying. In God's kindness, she is more teachable and even reaches out to seek our advice. She has never asked us for money nor has she asked to come back home. I admire her tenacity and her willingness to try again and again when she fails. We continue to seek God for guidance on how to help her become the independent adult she longs to be, and to find her own brand of success under the providential gaze of the Lord.

Some would argue that we should have the right to be bitter that God brought Jackie to us in the first place, only seemingly

---

1. 'But he said to me, "My grace is sufficient for you, for my power is made perfect in weakness." Therefore I will boast all the more gladly of my weaknesses, so that the power of Christ may rest upon me.'

to fail. But, I can proclaim without hesitation that I would not trade raising our precious daughter, not just because of the blessing it afforded her and our family, but because we would have never known the depth, the absolute reality of God's love and care had Jackie not come into our lives. The goodness of God includes His bringing us into the refining fires of trial and affliction. Our obedience does not guarantee ease and what we view as success. The outcome of obedience to the hard call of God is comfort in the midst of trial, clarity in the midst of confusion, and peace in the midst of chaos. So we trust Him, with Jackie, with our granddaughter, and, though it was not what we expected, the outcome of our circumstances. And with the psalmist, we can declare, 'Because your steadfast love is better than life, my lips will praise you' (Ps. 63:3).

Yet I Will Rejoice

To the parent who is at the end of things, and whose life with their mentally ill child screams louder than God's good promises, Habakkuk 3:17-19 offers this marvelous assurance:

> Though the fig tree should not blossom,
>   nor fruit be on the vines,
> the produce of the olive fail
>   and the fields yield no food,
> the flock be cut off from the fold
>   and there be no herd in the stalls,
> yet I will rejoice in the Lord;
>   I will take joy in the God of my salvation.
> God, the Lord, is my strength;
>   he makes my feet like the deer's;
>   he makes me tread on my high places.